Where Bernie Went Wrong

Where Bernie Went Wrong

And Why His Remedies Will Just Make Crony Capitalism Worse

Hunter Lewis

Axios Press
PO Box 457
Edinburg, VA 22824
888.542.9467   info@axiosinstitute.org

Publisher's Cataloging-in-Publication

    Lewis, Hunter, author.
    Where Bernie went wrong : and why his remedies will just make crony capitalism worse / Hunter Lewis.
    pages cm
    Includes bibliographical references and index.
    LCCN 2016949258
    ISBN 978-1-60419-108-0 (cloth)
    ISBN 978-1-60419-120-2 (paperback)
    ISBN 978-1-60419-109-7 (ebook)
    1. Sanders, Bernard--Political and social views. 2. Presidential candidates--United States--Biography. 3. Legislators--United States--Biography. 4. Socialism--United States. 5. Progressivism (United States politics) 6. United States--Politics and government--1989- 7. Biographies. I. Title.

E840.8.S26L49 2016

328.73'092

QBI16-900026

Contents

Preface

BERNIE SANDERS WON 13,618,214 votes in the Democratic primaries of 2016. Some of these votes may have reflected anti-Hillary sentiment. But many voters, even those not voting for him, seemed genuinely moved and inspired by what he had to say.

It is unlikely that Bernie ran hoping to win. It is more likely that he ran because it gave him a platform, and he wanted to use that platform to explain and propagate his views, especially among young people.

If Bernie's campaign was primarily an exercise in moving public opinion, it was wildly successful. He carried young people by wide margins. He shifted the Democratic Party and eventually its platform in his direction. It also resulted in Hillary Clinton eventually adopting virtually all of his major proposals. It had a tremendous impact on the election of 2016 and beyond.

Looking back on his campaign and its influence on American voters, especially young voters, we need to ask: how sound are Bernie's views? To what degree are they sound? To what degree are they backed by evidence, logic, and above all common sense? Trying to sort out these questions is the task of this short book.

Like any such effort, it will reflect the biases of the author. But with luck the factual evidence and at least some of the logic will speak for itself.

Where Bernie Went Wrong begins with some well-deserved tribute to a man who has devoted his life to improving our society. It notes how admirable and sincere that life has been. It proceeds to argue that Bernie's analysis of the failures of our society are largely accurate and his exposition of those failures powerful. Moreover, populism, a word with which he is often identified, when correctly defined as an unfailing focus on the poor and the middle class, is exactly what this country needs.

At the same time, his proposed solutions are not new, despite his repeated claims that they are. In this respect, he seems to be deceiving himself rather than prevaricating. His views are very old, at least a century old, dating all the way back to the Fabian Socialism of late nineteenth century Britain, and ultimately back much further than that, as we will show.

His favored solutions have been frequently tried, so there is evidence as well as logic available to evaluate them. And in general, they do not pass the test. They are not well supported by evidence, logic, or common sense. They will not help us cope with or improve on current reality, because they are too much grounded in wishful thinking rather than reality.

There are real solutions, the best of them populist solutions, for the serious problems that Bernie eloquently describes. But Bernie's approach of giving government even more power and responsibility for the economy will just make matters worse, and in particular lead to more political corruption. That is the thesis of this book, and readers can decide for themselves whether the case is successfully made.

This is not the kind of book that will earn five stars on Amazon, Google, or Goodreads. Readers who agree may give it five stars; those who disagree are likely to respond angrily or dismissively by giving it one star at best. This is too bad. It is especially intended for those who may be inclined to refuse to read it or consider its arguments.

We all need to evaluate and discuss Bernie's ideas, most of them now adopted by Hillary Clinton and the rest of the Democratic Party, as calmly, deliberately, and objectively as we can. His ideas are unquestionably important.

Norman Thomas, the Socialist Party candidate for president in 1932, said that he did not need to keep running, because President Roosevelt had adopted all his ideas. This was largely true. The same has happened with Bernie's ideas in the Democratic Party. But if this book is correct, they have the potential to harm the very poor and middle class that Bernie so ardently wants to help.

Part One

Getting to Know Him

1

Where Is Bernie Coming From?

BERNIE IS EASY to like, even admire. Dressed in rumpled clothes, with wisps of tussled white hair, the septuagenarian appears to be the grandfather we all wish we had. He is not an eloquent or powerful speaker, but exudes sincerity.

Very few politicians are willing to tell us what they really believe or what they will actually do in office, but this man does. No one need fear being deceived. By contrast, Hillary Clinton, his primary opponent, gets her lowest ratings from voters for "honesty" and "trustworthiness."

At various times, he has referred to himself as a "socialist," a "democratic socialist," and a "progressive." He seems to use these terms more or less interchangeably. Both his accent and his ideas reveal a working class origin in Brooklyn long ago, further shaped by long residence in Burlington, Vermont.

Bernie lives in a modest home. He does not vacation on Martha's Vineyard or the Hamptons with the rich and famous. It is clear that he has not enriched himself by public service.

This is not only in sharp contrast to Hillary Clinton, but also to other leading Democratic leaders such as former Senate Majority Leader Harry Reid, former Speaker of the House Nancy Pelosi, and Vice President Joe Biden, all of whom have become very wealthy through real estate and other deals supplied by political friends and backers. Biden refers to himself as "middle class Joe," but would seem to be anything but. Sanders truly is middle class in outlook, income, and assets, and has never sought to be anything else.

When Sanders describes himself as a "socialist," he clarifies that government should not abolish private property, but should take the principal role in leading and governing the economy. For most of his political life, he has run as an "independent," but in the US Senate has "caucused" with the Democrats and in effect acted as one of them. He eventually chose to run for President as a Democrat.

His life story is compelling. Here is what he says about it:

> Brothers and sisters, throughout history, for whatever reason (and I'm not a psychiatrist) racism has

been a stain on human existence. . . . I lost many members of my family in Europe to Hitler.

National Council of La Raza, August 12, 2015

My father came to this country from Poland at the age of 17 without a penny in his pocket, [without speaking English,] and without much of an education. My mother graduated from high school in New York City. My father worked for almost his entire life as a paint salesman and we lived with my brother in a small rent-controlled apartment [in Brooklyn]. My mother's dream was to move out of that three-room apartment into a home of our own. She died young and her dream was never fulfilled. As a kid I learned what lack of money means to a family, and I also never liked to see people without a lot of wealth put down or pushed around. That is why when I was elected Mayor [of Burlington] and then went on to Congress I tried every day to be a voice for people who did not have a voice.

Des Moines, Iowa, June 12, 2015

[My father] worked hard, my mom worked hard, and they were able to create a situation where their two kids went to college.

Fair Immigration Reform Movement
Strategy Summit, November 9, 2015

When I was a young college student, I came to Washington, DC, to participate in the March on

Washington for Jobs and Freedom. I heard this organization's first president, the Rev. Martin Luther King, Jr., deliver his famous speech, and he inspired me, just as he inspired a whole generation—black and white—to get involved in the civil rights movement. In Chicago, I worked for housing desegregation and was arrested protesting public school segregation. During that time I was active in what was a sister-organization to the SCLC, the Congress of Racial Equality or CORE, which was headed up by the late James Farmer.

Southern Christian Leadership Conference,
July 25, 2015

What Dr. King saw in 1968—and what we all should recognize today—is that it is not enough to address race alone without also taking on the larger issue of inequality. Let us not forget that when Dr. King was assassinated he was fighting to improve the wages and working conditions of sanitation workers who were on strike in Memphis, Tennessee.

National Urban League, July 31, 2015

I was mayor of Burlington, Vermont, from 1981–1989, Vermont's lone congressman from 1990–2006 and a US senator from Vermont from 2007 until today.

National Urban League, July 31, 2015

I have seen the promise of America in my own life. My parents would have never dreamed that their son would be a US Senator, let alone run for President.

Waterfront Park, Burlington, Vermont,
May 26, 2015

The decision to run for president was a very difficult one for me and my family. I love my job as Vermont's senator and love spending time in Vermont with my four kids and seven beautiful grandchildren.

Southern Christian Leadership Conference,
July 25, 2015

I want to thank my family: my wife Jane, my brother Larry, my children Levi, Heather, Carina, and Dave for their love and support, and my seven beautiful grandchildren—Sonny, Cole, Ryleigh, Grayson, Ella, Tess, and Dylan who provide so much joy in my life.

Waterfront Park, Burlington, Vermont,
May 26, 2015

We have, I believe, received more individual campaign contributions than any other presidential campaign, some 400,000. And in this day of super-PACs and huge campaign contributions, I am proud to tell you that our average contribution is $31.20.

Democratic National Committee, August 28, 2015

Let's be clear. This campaign is not about Bernie Sanders. It is . . . about the needs of the American

people. . . . As someone who has never run a negative political ad in his life, my campaign will be driven
by issues and serious debate; not political gossip,
not reckless personal attacks or character assassi-
nation. This is what I believe the American people
want and deserve. I hope other candidates agree,
and I hope the media allows that to happen. Politics in a democratic society should not be treated
like a baseball game, a game show, or a soap opera.

Waterfront Park, Burlington, Vermont,
May 26, 2015

2

What Bernie Gets (Very!) Right

BERNIE OFTEN SAYS out loud what others are privately thinking. This is especially true for those of us who regard ourselves as populists, in the sense that we want what will be best for everyone, not just the elite, and especially best for the poor and the middle class of this country. Here are some examples. The words are not always fluent or eloquent, but the sentiments are obviously heartfelt:

> Brothers and sisters, the fact of the matter is that there is a war going on in this country today. And, I'm not talking about the misguided and unnecessary war we waged in Iraq.
>
> I'm talking about the 40-year war against the American middle class, the American standard of living, and the American dream of owning a home, sending kids to college, and having a secure retirement.
>
> AFL-CIO Conference, August 18, 2015

The bottom line is that today in America we not only have massive wealth and income inequality, but a power structure which protects that inequality.*

> On Democratic Socialism in the United States,
> November 19, 2015

Democratic socialism means that we must reform a political system in America today which is not only grossly unfair but, in many respects, corrupt.

. . . It means that we create a government that works for all of us, not just powerful special interests.

> On Democratic Socialism in the United States,
> November 19, 2015

Now, the truth is that no president, not Bernie Sanders, or anybody else, can do what it takes to rebuild the middle class alone. . . .

We need a political revolution. We need millions of Americans to begin to stand up and fight back and demand a government that represents all of us.

> United Steelworkers Rally, April 29, 2016

If these were normal times many people in our country could be supportive of Establishment politics,

---

* Whether economic inequality is bad in itself, to what degree, and under what circumstances, will be discussed in subsequent chapters. Senator Sanders's larger point is that the deck is stacked against the middle class and the poor.

Establishment economics and Establishment foreign policy. But these are not normal times. And what I see from coast to coast is an American people crying out for change, for real change. They do not want the same-old, same-old.

New Hampshire Democratic Party
Jefferson-Jackson Dinner, November 29, 2015

We can deliver . . . change, but we can't do it by tinkering with the system at the margins. We need to think bigger and bolder if we are going to deliver the kind of social and economic transformation that we are all demanding.

Presidential Justice Forum at Allen University,
November 21, 2015

I am told time and time again by the rich and powerful, and the mainstream media that represent them, that we should be "practical," that we should accept the status quo; that a truly moral economy is beyond our reach.

The Urgency of a Moral Economy: Reflections
on the 25th Anniversary of Centesimus Annus,
April 15, 2016

It would, I think, be hard for anyone in this room to make the case that the United States today is a "just" society or anything resembling a just society.

We need to move toward an economy which works for all, and not just the few.

I would hope very much that . . . some of you will conclude that if we strive toward morality and toward justice, it is imperative that we have the courage to stand with the poor and working people of our country.

Liberty University Convocation, September 14, 2015

I am running for president because we live in . . . a very rigged economy—the rich get much richer while almost everybody else becomes poorer.

New Hampshire Democratic Party
Jefferson-Jackson Dinner, November 29, 2015

It is the tragic reality that for the last 40 years the great middle class of our country—once the envy of the world—has been disappearing. Despite exploding technology and increased worker productivity, median family income is almost $5,000 less than it was in 1999. Throughout this country it is not uncommon for people to be working two or three jobs just to cobble together enough income and some healthcare benefits to survive.

Des Moines, Iowa, June 12, 2015

Despite the incredibly hard work and long hours of the American middle class, 58 percent of all new income generated today is going to the top one percent. *

On Democratic Socialism in the United States,
November 19, 2015

---

* Recent Economic Policy Institute Study says it is not 58% but rather 85% since the Crash of 2008. Bernie's figure may be a typo.

It is unacceptable that the typical male worker made $783 less last year than he did 42 years ago. . . . It is unacceptable that the typical female worker made $1,337 less last year than she did in 2007.

AFL-CIO Conference, August 18, 2015

Today, in America, the wealthiest country in the history of the world, more than half of older workers have no retirement savings—zero—while millions of elderly and people with disabilities are trying to survive on $12,000 or $13,000 a year. . . .

Today, in America, nearly 47 million Americans are living in poverty and over 20 percent of our children, including 36 percent of African-American children, are living in poverty—the highest rate of childhood poverty of nearly any major country on earth.

Today, in America, 29 million Americans have no health insurance and even more are underinsured with outrageously high co-payments and deductibles.

On Democratic Socialism in the United States,
November 19, 2015

Real unemployment in America is not 5.3 percent, it is 10.5 percent. [Note: arguably it is even higher.] And the real tragedy . . . is youth unemployment. Kids between the ages of 17 to 20 who have graduated high school: if they are white their unemployment rate is 33 percent, if they are Hispanic 36 percent, if they are African-American 51 percent.

In other words we are turning our backs on an entire generation of young people.

July 29 Organizing Kickoff Event, July 29, 2015

Today we [also] have millions of young people and people who are not so young who are struggling with outrageously high student debt. And they are carrying this debt for decades in some cases. In fact I talked to a woman a while back, she's paying off her debt, she's paying off her daughter's debt. That's really not all that uncommon.

July 29 Organizing Kickoff Event, July 29, 2015

We—the United States of America—[also] have more people in jail than any other country on earth. We have more people in jail than China which is an authoritarian state with a population many times our own. And we should lay it all right out on the table. People in American jails are disproportionately people of color. That's the reality in America today. That's a reality that has to change.

Presidential Justice Forum at Allen University, November 21, 2015

One in every 15 African-American men is incarcerated, compared to one in every 106 white men. . . . Thirteen percent of African-American men have lost the right to vote due to felony convictions.

Presidential Justice Forum at Allen University, November 21, 2015

We must end the over incarceration of non-violent young Americans who do not pose a serious threat to our society.

We must address the lingering unjust stereotypes that lead us to label black youths as "thugs" and "super-predators." We must . . . keep kids in school. We must ensure that children graduate from high school and don't drop out.

Presidential Justice Forum at Allen University,
November 21, 2015

We also have to develop standards and crack down on communities that are using their police forces essentially as revenue generators. . . . Communities that receive an inordinate amount of their local funding through fines and citations need to be stopped.

Presidential Justice Forum at Allen University,
November 21, 2015

We have to make sure poor communities have access to credit on fair terms, so they can buy homes, start business, and avoid predatory lenders.

Presidential Justice Forum at Allen University,
November 21, 2015

Our foreign policy, for the last many decades, has failed the American people, has led to wars, like the war in Iraq, which we should never have gotten into. Now is not the time for more establishment foreign policy.

New Hampshire Democratic Party
Jefferson-Jackson Dinner, November 29, 2015

There is another issue out there that is so enormous and it touches all of us as adults and those of us who are parents, and that is the moral responsibility we have to leave this planet in a habitable way for our children and our grandchildren.

July 29 Organizing Kickoff Event, July 29, 2015

Part Two

What Bernie Gets
Half Right

3

Bernie against "Corruption" and a "Rigged Economy"

AS NOTED IN chapter two, Bernie argues that:

> We must reform a political system in America today which is not only grossly unfair but, in many respects, corrupt.
>
> On Democratic Socialism in the United States,
> November 19, 2015

This political corruption leads to what he frequently refers to as a rigged economy:

> I am running for president because we live in the wealthiest nation in the history of the world but that reality means little to most Americans because—in a very rigged economy—the rich get much richer while almost everybody else becomes poorer.
>
> New Hampshire Democratic Party
> Jefferson-Jackson Dinner, November 29, 2015

The economy becomes rigged because the rich, primarily represented by "greedy" billionaires and corporations, use their wealth to subvert the political process and take command of government. The most notorious corporate subverters operate a few specific industries:

> Since I have been an elected official, I have used my influence to stand with those who have no power, and to take on virtually every element of our current ruling class—from Wall Street, to the insurance companies, to the drug companies to Big Energy, to the Koch Brothers to the Military Industrial Complex. That's what I do.
>
> Southern Christian Leadership Conference,
> July 25, 2015

Here is an example of how the subversion works:

> During the 1990s [the current system] . . . allowed Wall Street to spend $5 billion in lobbying and campaign contributions to get deregulated. Then, ten years later, after the greed, recklessness, and illegal behavior of Wall Street led to their collapse, it is a system which provided trillions in government aid to bail them out. . . . Quite a system!
>
> On Democratic Socialism in the United States,
> November 19, 2015

Bernie has a very good point here. It does not seem so much a capitalist system in the United States as a crony capitalist system in which individuals get rich, not by supplying good products and services at the lowest possible cost for consumers, but rather by getting monopoly protections or other favors from government or by otherwise benefiting from government actions or connections. This is not just in the US. It is perhaps worst in Russia and China today, but it seems to be getting steadily worse in the US.

For example, Goldman Sachs, a major Wall Street firm threatened with bankruptcy during the Crash of 2008 not only got a direct bailout from the government. Even more importantly, its friends in Washington arranged for the firm, a notorious Wall Street speculator, to be redefined as a bank, so that it could borrow vast amounts of money from the Federal Reserve at virtually no interest.

Who were these friends? One of them was the man in charge of the bailout, Hank Paulson, Secretary of the Treasury, former CEO of Goldman, and owner of large quantities of Goldman stock. This was a gift of billions of dollars to Goldman, handled as stealthily as possible, and virtually invisible to the press, under pretense of a loan from the Fed.

The money made available in this way was all newly created, produced "out of thin air" by the Fed through the flick of an electronic keyboard. It could be used for whatever purpose the firm wished, including more of the speculation and unethical conduct that had gotten it in trouble in the first place. And the ability

to borrow from the Fed at virtually no interest continues to this day.

Looking at this kind of evidence, Bernie would seem
to be right. His account is partially right, but incomplete. For one thing, he describes government being
subverted by greedy billionaires and companies, but
gives government officials a free pass. Are not government officials also guilty for letting themselves be
seduced and subverted? Bernie never points the finger
at anyone in government, and there is a reason for this
glaring omission on his part.

Bernie proposes to solve the problem of political
corruption and a rigged economy by giving government even more power. How will this help? Surely an
expanded and even more powerful government, ever
more deeply involved in running the economy, will
become an even more tempting target for the wealthy
subverters?

If the subverters have been tempted by the billions
to be made by subverting government in the past, and
largely successful in doing so, would it not become a
matter of sheer survival for them to subvert and control the all-powerful government that Bernie wants?
Are not Bernie's ideas self-contradictory? How can we
possibly solve crony capitalism by increasing the oppor-
tunities and rewards for crony capitalism? Surely there
must be a better way of tackling the very real problems
that the Senator describes?

Bernie is silent about this, so one can only guess how he would respond. Perhaps he thinks, as many fellow progressives do, that government officials are inherently virtuous, and that by giving them more power, they will call a halt to the corruption and refuse to be so easily subverted by moneyed interests.

The problem with this idea is that government officials are human beings. They have their own goals quite apart from their role as public servants. For example, if elected, they want to be re-elected.

Re-election costs money, which private interest can supply. As we shall see, Bernie decries this and wants government funding of elections, but this has the potential to backfire as well, because it can be used to the advantage of incumbents. Nor do elected officials only want to be re-elected. Some of them may also exploit office for money or, as in the case of Bill Clinton, for sex.

In addition to the enrichment by private interests of Vice President Joe Biden, former Speaker of the House Nancy Pelosi, and former Majority Leader Harry Reid, there are many other such stories. President Obama borrowed money to buy his Chicago mansion from a man who was subsequently convicted and jailed for political corruption. His closest advisor in the White House, Valerie Jarrett, reportedly got rich from a real estate deal combined with a big local tax break while serving as chief of staff to the mayor of Chicago. These stories do not speak well of American democracy.

If working in regulatory bodies, public officials want raises or bonuses, to enjoy financial perks, and in many cases to land a much higher paying job in the industries they are supposed to regulate. Elected officials may also angle for future jobs that will make them rich.

At the Food and Drug Administration, which controls much of the US economy, the agency is directly funded by the companies that are supposed to be regulated. Is it a surprise that FDA officials seem to view themselves as employees or at least allies of the regulated drug companies, not as regulators working for the public?

Surely, if we are going to do something about crony capitalism, we had better admit that the corruption involves government officials as well as their wealthy would-be subverters. And there are some other problems with Bernie's account, as we shall discuss in the next chapter.

4

Bernie against
Special Interests

As NOTED IN the prior chapter, there are two sides of the crony capitalist coin: predatory special interests and pliant government officials who are willing to be bought or at least rented. More often than not, rented is the correct word, because as Ugandan dictator Idi Amin once explained in a television interview, "in politics there are no permanent friends and no permanent enemies." Bernie conveniently ignores all this, but agrees that special interest political power must be curbed:

> Democratic socialism . . . means that we create a government that works for all of us, not just powerful special interests.
>
> On Democratic Socialism in the United States,
> November 19, 2015

Sanders further says that the way to beat special interests is to mobilize the "grassroots":

> The powers that be, that is corporate America, Wall Street, the insurance companies, the drug companies, the military industrial complex, these guys are enormously powerful. And the only way that we can defeat them, the only way we can transform America, the only way we can have a government which begins to work for working people rather than the wealthiest people in this country is by putting together an unprecedentedly strong grassroots movement, and what I call a political revolution.
>
> July 29 Organizing Kickoff Event, July 29, 2015

This sounds reasonable, but again something is missing. Bernie only names special interests that have either contributed to the other party, the Republicans, or, more commonly, have contributed to both parties. He omits any mention of special interests that traditionally provide massive funding for, or mostly for, the Democratic Party, notably trade unions and trial lawyers.

This is not an inadvertent slip. In Bernie's world view, the special interests that support him cannot be called special interests, no matter how much they seek to influence or win favors from government. This position is more or less taken for granted by Bernie. He neither acknowledges nor tries to defend it.

Despite his taking it for granted, Bernie's position does not seem to pass any kind of logical test. If one opposes crony capitalism, and if, as part of that, one opposes special interests getting access to and favors from government, then it seems that one should oppose all special interests operating this way, not just some, not just those that do not contribute to your campaign, and exempt those which do.

Bernie says:

> I am a proud progressive, prepared to stand with the working families of this country; prepared to take on powerful special interests which wield enormous power over the economic and political life of this country.
>
> New Hampshire Democratic Party Convention,
> September 19, 2015

Based on his remarks and record, however, Bernie will not stand with working Americans against corrupt unions, even when they are stealing from their members or trying to get control of government. Nor will he stand against parasitical trial lawyers intent on threatening and demanding protection money from every industry and thereby raising prices on almost everything for everyone.

There is something else arguably illogical about Bernie's idea of special interests. Although he says he is for all Americans and especially all working people, he is perfectly comfortable making special appeals to certain groups of voters, who themselves may represent political special interests. For example, he says to a Latino group:

> I'm proud to stand with the Latino community and
> receive a 100% voting score from the National His-
> panic Leadership Agenda last Congress.
>
> National Association of Latino Elected and Ap-
> pointed Officials Conference, June 19, 2015

Is the National Hispanic Leadership Agenda always
100% compatible with what is best for all Americans?

In the same speech, Bernie added that:

> Martin Luther King, Jr. reminded us [that we should
> consider people] . . . not on the color of their skin,
> not on the language they speak, not on the coun-
> try where they came from, but on their character
> and qualities as human beings.
>
> National Council of La Raza, August 12, 2015

But Bernie's own approach does not really seem consistent with Martin Luther King's. It is anything but
skin color or ethnicity blind.

Sometimes Bernie's outreach (we will not call it pandering) to special voter groups teeters on the comical.
Here, for example, he is speaking to Latinos:

> [When] speculation and illegal behavior plunged
> this country into the worst financial crisis since the
> 1930s [in 2008], . . . Latinos were the hardest hit.
> Latinos were disproportionately steered into sub-
> prime loans.
>
> National Association of Latino Elected and Ap-
> pointed Officials Conference, June 19, 2015

Now he is speaking to an African-American group:

> [Following the Crash of 2008,] . . . African-Americans who were steered into expensive subprime mortgages were the hardest hit.

> National Urban League, July 31, 2015

So who was hardest hit? Latinos or African-Americans? Perhaps this was just a careless staff member's error, when he or she was asked to adapt old remarks for the next group. But the contradiction remains on Sanders's website.

And does it really matter which racial or ethnic group was hardest hit by the Crash of 2008? Weren't all Americans hard hit by the collusion of Wall Street and government that took place (yes, both Wall Street and government were working together as we shall document in a subsequent chapter), and is it not what happened to all Americans, especially all poor or middle class Americans, especially the most vulnerable Americans, that matters?

5

Bernie for Unions

THERE IS NO doubt that unions are Bernie's very favorite special interest, although he prefers not to acknowledge that they are a special interest, and one of the most powerful at that. If we are going to overcome or at least try to control crony capitalism, it will not help to rein in some special interests, while encouraging other special interests to grow fatter and fatter off their relationship with government.

Of course, it is part of progressive political legend that unions are just groups of workers trying to protect themselves from rapacious private employers. But this is hardly a reliable account of today's reality. Most unionized workers today are employed by government, not by private companies.

Not long ago, progressive leaders such as Woodrow Wilson and Franklin Roosevelt took the position that public employees should never be allowed to unionize. They preferred to think of government simply as "the people" (yet another myth contradicted by the crony capitalist reality), and insisted that workers should never be allowed collectively to bargain with "the people," much less be allowed to strike.

President John F. Kennedy changed much of that in the early 1960s by executive order. He thought that authorizing public employee unions would produce a torrent of campaign contributions for the Democratic Party, and he was absolutely right about that. He did not, however, allow federal employees to strike, only to represent employees in contract talks. That is why the airplane traffic controllers' strike at the start of the Reagan administration was illegal, which allowed Reagan to take the surprising step of firing the strikers and replacing them.

Bernie has not advocated giving public unions the right to strike, but he does want an expansion of their right to bargain collectively:

> We need to expand collective bargaining rights for private sector and public sector workers.
>
> United Steelworkers Rally, April 29, 2016

Public unions take dues from members regardless of those members' political views or preferences, and reliably, almost invariably, deliver millions of these dollars to Democrats. This in turn greatly increases the incentive of Democrats to expand government departments and thus increase this flow of dues into politics.

The US Post Office has for decades lost increasing amounts of money while service steadily slipped. UPS and Fed Ex proved that mail delivery services could be efficiently handled by private companies, but the idea of closing the Post Office has always been a non-starter precisely because it would stop millions of dollars of dues money going each year to the Democratic Party.

After the terrorist destruction of the Twin Towers in New York on 9/11/2001, a new department of Homeland Security was established. One of the questions to be sorted out by Congress was whether airport screeners would work for private companies, as they do in Europe, or only for the government. The Democratic Party was adamant that the airport staff had to be government employees, because they wanted the assured political contributions that would result.

Bernie endorses the right of unions to take money from members and use it politically without that member's consent. He has misrepresented attempts by states to give members a say about whether they contribute to politics through the union:

> That's why [right wing politicians] have fought so hard to eliminate unions in Wisconsin, Indiana, Ohio, Michigan, and all over this country by ending collective bargaining rights.
>
> AFL-CIO Conference, August 18, 2015

This is not what happened. Wisconsin did restrict collective bargaining rights of teachers among other steps. But efforts to allow workers to decide whether to join the union or (if they do join the union) whether to allow their dues to be used by union bosses for political purposes are not necessarily or even primarily an attempt to end collective bargaining. It is instead an attempt to reduce political corruption and also to restore fiscal sanity.

Governors and mayors who are receiving large political campaign contributions from unions cannot possibly be expected to bargain with them objectively over wages. Here is just one example. Jon Corzine was a major donor to the Democratic Party and a Wall Streeter who had led Goldman Sachs before leaving to become senator from and then governor of New Jersey. While governor he told a union audience that he would "fight for you" during contract negotiations.

This rhetoric was utterly ridiculous since the negotiations were with the governor, allegedly representing the interests of the people of New Jersey. After failing in his re-election bid, Corzine's new firm on Wall Street went spectacularly bankrupt during the Crash of 2008, with charges of misappropriated funds, but no charges were ever filed against this friend and confidante of President Obama's. When the Crash began, Obama said that the first person he called for advice was Corzine!

Interestingly, when union workers are allowed to decide whether their dues can be involuntarily used for political purposes, a majority often votes no. It is not lost on them that most union political activism does not even directly relate to working conditions, but rather supports the entire Democratic Party agenda, which many workers do not support.

Bernie of course does not mention any of this. He always describes unions in glowingly mythical terms. When union policies clash with other ideas of his, the contradiction is simply ignored. For example, Bernie has proposed major changes in how policing is done in black communities. But chiefs of police who try to implement any such ideas have often been thwarted by union rules and contracts. It is hard to implement any reforms in policing when the chief of police does not even have the power to fire police officers.

In Bernie's world view, unions not only help union members; they help everyone, a claim that we will further discuss below. He also takes whatever money he can get from them and in return they can count on him to support their government agenda:

> I want to thank all of the 12.5 million members of the AFL-CIO for working hard each and every day to improve the lives of all of the American people.

> AFL-CIO Conference, August 18, 2015

Bernie adds that:

> [Billionaires and greedy companies] . . . under-
> stand that the major obstacle standing in the way
> of their extreme, right wing agenda is the trade
> union movement.
>
> AFL-CIO Conference, August 18, 2015

If this is true, then Bernie is really saying that the only thing controlling one set of special interests is another set of special interests, and that voters are virtually powerless. Yet on most occasions, he seems to be saying the opposite, that the voters can and must take back control of government.

When Bernie discusses his own campaign's financing, he proudly mentions the remarkable outpouring of small, individual gifts he received. This is indeed worth celebrating. Who would not prefer for candidates to be supported by large numbers of small gifts, especially if they come from a broad cross section of the public, not just narrow voter interest groups or large, special interest groups. But why does not Bernie admit that, in fact, he has taken large donations from unions?

> We have, I believe, received more individual cam-
> paign contributions than any other presidential cam-
> paign . . . I do not represent the corporate agenda
> or the billionaire class—and I do not want their
> money and I do not and will not have a Super-PAC.
>
> New Hampshire Democratic Party Convention,
> September 19, 2015

This is all true, but incomplete. As previously noted, refusing money from billionaires, companies, and Super-PACS does not mean refusing money from all special interests. Many billionaire donors are Democrats, as we shall discuss later. Did Bernie receive donations from any of them? Perhaps not. Perhaps they were all supporting Hillary Clinton. But would he have refused a donation from a Tom Steyer or a George Soros if offered? We do not know.

Bernie also asks:

> How did it happen that since 2001, over 60,000 factories have shut down in America and millions of good-paying manufacturing jobs have disappeared?
>
> AFL-CIO Conference, August 18, 2015

This is a good question. But it is not just because greedy companies took the jobs overseas. In many cases, these companies have taken jobs overseas in order to survive, and by surviving have by definition employed more Americans than they otherwise would have if no longer in business.

Economic effects are hard to understand because, as economic writer Henry Hazlitt pointed out, many of them are seen (loss of jobs that moved overseas) while others are unseen (ability to create new US jobs from the resulting company revenue). In addition, effects may be short term (again closing of a US plant) but others take time to play out (new US hiring because of the overseas production). This does not necessarily mean that Bernie is wrong, and we will discuss this further later in this book. But he is over-simplifying.

Bernie never mentions that companies have been driven overseas by their union's refusal to face the reality of global economic competition. This may, however, be because, in Bernie's mind, we could eliminate global competition with more tariffs, a subject we will also get to later in the book, but for now suffice it to say that there are reasons to doubt this could succeed or would not result in an even greater loss of jobs.

General Motors has been a notorious example of a company that paid higher and higher wages to its unionized employees (usually in return for being allowed to shrink the workforce) and that mostly stayed in the US to avoid a crippling strike, only to face bankruptcy as a result. What happened then was highly illustrative of how crony capitalism works.

The Obama administration was not going to let GM go bankrupt for at least two reasons. First that would cut off the flow of campaign contributions from the United Auto Workers. Perhaps even more importantly, GM employees were concentrated in Ohio and Pennsylvania, both key swing states in presidential elections. Neither the Democrats nor the GOP dared alienate those key swing voters.

As soon as GM announced that it was going bankrupt, President Bush stepped in to buy time. President

Obama then engineered a bailout that transferred a majority stake in the company to union hands. The very union that had laid GM low through its unwillingness to face the reality of competition from foreign car makers not only ended up in complete control, but was also enabled to make a killing off the sale of shares it had been given.

Meanwhile the Obama administration insisted that the GM bondholders not receive a dime, even though most of the bondholders by then were retired individuals of very modest means. They had wrongly assumed that GM was one of the very safest places for their retirement money. The stories of the financial hardships these old people faced as a result were heartbreaking. They should have at least gotten something back, but instead were robbed so that the union could get everything.

What the Obama administration did violated bankruptcy law, but which of these small bondholders had the money to sue? The Obama administration even arranged for the vehicles warranty holders to lose every penny still remaining on their warranties. The government figured that these people would never know that their money too went to the union, and the press gave it very little coverage, almost no coverage of the administration's role in forcing this result.

Bernie also strongly endorses the idea, voiced above, that unions help all workers, not just the members, and indeed all Americans:

> The trade union movement has always led the fight to improve the quality of life for all Americans, and that is what the AFL-CIO is all about. . . .
>
> We know that union workers earn 30 percent more money, on average, than non-union workers. If you want to make more money to support your family, you need a union!
>
> AFL-CIO Conference, August 18, 2015

The problem with this argument is that gains of unionized workers do not come out of an employer's profits. They come out of other workers' wages. This is a technical topic little understood even by most economists, but can be briefly explained as follows.

When workers unionize and this leads to higher wages, their employer will try to economize by automating or otherwise hiring fewer people, just as General Motors attempted to do. As fewer people will be employed in the unionized sector, the number of people looking for work outside will be increased. The law of supply and demand means that, all else being equal, an increase in the supply of labor in non-unionized sectors will reduce wages there. Overall, the share of labor will not increase.

Nor will the total profits of business owners be reduced. The company with the union may indeed suffer lower profits. But the unionized workers will have more money to spend on goods and services, and the producers of those goods and services will sell more.

So even if one employer has reduced profits, employers as a whole will not be affected.

Bernie might respond that this could be solved by requiring the unionization of all workers. But this is not likely to be feasible, even if we were not in a global market. In addition, some unions would be stronger than others, which would produce the same effect of worker inequality.

We must also keep in mind that a completely unionized world would be much more resistant to economic change, which is ultimately the source of business profits, which over time are the only source of new hiring and worker raises. The bottom line: Bernie does not seem to understand economics, or else lets his wishes dominate his logic.

Finally Bernie offers the fable that unionized workers have better pension plans:

> We know that 79 percent of union workers have a defined benefit pension plan that guarantees income in retirement, while only 16 percent of non-union workers do. If you want to have a secure retirement, you need a union!
>
> AFL-CIO Conference, August 18, 2015

This claim falls far short on the fact test. Union pension funds have been riddled by corruption, misspent and misused over the years, and are today as a rule massively underfunded. The guarantee of one of these pension funds is about as reliable as GM's promise to pay its bondholders and warranty holders.

It is also ironic that the efforts of the US government's Federal Reserve to hold down government interest rates to near zero levels since the collapse of the dot-com bubble, and especially since the collapse of the housing bubble, have especially injured defined benefit pension plans of the kind offered by unions, in addition to other defined benefit plans, and insurance products of all kinds, including retirement policies. It is all too likely that many of these plans will collapse in the future, not only from poor management, but also from misguided government economic policies.

Part Three

The Rich

6

Bernie against Billionaires

O NE OF BERNIE'S principal themes, reiterated over and over in speech after speech, is that we must take back government from the billionaires.

> Our government should belong to all of us and not as is currently the case, a hand-full of billionaires.
>
> July 29 Organizing Kickoff Event, July 29, 2015

Overstated perhaps, but most Americans would surely agree.

> If we are serious about transforming our country, if we are serious about rebuilding the middle class, if we are serious about reinvigorating our democracy, we need to develop a political movement which, once again, is prepared to take on and defeat a ruling class whose greed is destroying our nation. The

> billionaire class cannot have it all. Our government
> belongs to all of us, and not just the one percent.
>
> On Democratic Socialism in the United States,
> November 19, 2015

It is not entirely clear in this passage whether Bernie literally means billionaires, since in the same breath he refers to the top one percent. The top one percent usually refers to the 1% of Americans with the highest incomes. The cut-off for this category based on the most recent IRS data figure is $389,000 a year in family income.

Ironically top 1% income families in the US are especially concentrated in the counties surrounding Washington, DC. Six of the top ten counties for high income are found there and thirteen of the top thirty, according to the *Atlantic Magazine*.

Nor should this be surprising. It is not unusual for a couple, both of whom work for the government, to qualify. And of course many families reach that threshold not by working directly for the government, but by providing services to it. Because the government grew so much faster than private industry during the Bush and Obama administrations, this kind of direct and indirect work for it became arguably the single largest growth industry.

At other times, Bernie seems concerned about an "oligarchy" of millionaires as well as billionaires:

> I am running for president because we need an
> economy that works for working families, not just
> for millionaires and billionaires.
>
> New Hampshire Democratic Party
> Jefferson-Jackson Dinner, November 29, 2015

This is a rather broad brush. Does it not matter how the billionaires or millionaires got rich? Does it not matter if they got rich by meeting the needs of consumers versus getting rich through government supported monopolies or connections to public officials?

Even if the rich person's money was inherited, some of these distinctions apply. Are the rich investing in a way that helps the economy, and thereby creates jobs and provides better products or services at lower prices for consumers? Are they contributing to charity? Or are they just spending their money on undeserved personal luxuries?

Sometimes Bernie speaks of billionaires when he seems to mean companies. Although some companies are owned by billionaires, most are not:

> You can't continue sending our jobs to China while
> millions are looking for work. . . . Your greed has
> got to end. You cannot take advantage of all the
> benefits of America, if you refuse to accept your
> responsibilities as Americans.
>
> Des Moines, Iowa, June 12, 2015

He also occasionally tends to get so overheated when the word billionaires comes up that his rhetoric soars into a fact free zone:

> Let's be clear about what we are up against. . . .
>
> What do the Koch brothers want? Let me tell you.
>
> The Koch brothers and their billionaire allies don't just want to cut Social Security, they want to eliminate Social Security; they don't want to just cut Medicare, they want to eliminate Medicare; they don't just want to cut healthcare at the VA, they want to eliminate the Veterans Administration; they don't want to just cut the Postal Service, they want to eliminate it. . . .
>
> In other words, the Koch brothers and the billionaire class . . . want to give Americans the "freedom" to live in poverty working for $3 or $4 an hour without healthcare, without childcare, without a pension, without the ability to send their kids to college, and without any hope that their children will have a higher standard of living than they do.
>
> AFL-CIO Conference, August 18, 2015

This particular attack is not well supported by the record. The Kochs may want to abolish the Veterans Administration or the Post Office, but many others do as well, because these are failed organizations. The Kochs presumably hope to replace them with something that will work better.

Nor is there is any evidence that the Koch brothers want people to live in poverty earning $3 or $4 an hour with no health care or hope for retirement. On the contrary, their ideas, like Bernie's, right or wrong, have the stated goal of ending the stagnation of American wages, restoring a vibrant middle class, and abolishing poverty. As noted previously, Bernie also attacks billionaires whose political views do not match his own, but is silent about billionaires like Tom Steyer or George Soros contributing millions to the Democratic Party, if not to his own campaign.

Bernie is particularly concerned that recent Supreme Court rulings have greatly increased the power of the oligarchs to "buy" elections:

> As a result of the disastrous Supreme Court decision in the Citizens United case [in particular], the American political system has been totally corrupted, and the foundations of American democracy are being undermined. What the Supreme Court essentially said was that it was not good enough for the billionaire class to own much of our economy. They could now own the US government as well. And that is precisely what they are trying to do.
>
> AFL-CIO Conference, August 18, 2015

Bernie has reiterated this in many speeches, but note that the preceding remarks were delivered to an AFL-CIO Conference. The irony here is that unions have both been exempted from anti-trust rules and allowed to contribute to political campaigns ever since the Roosevelt administration. The Citizens United Case enraged Democrats because it leveled the playing field between companies and unions, while expanding the potential for both to participate in politics.

Bernie has a good case to make that companies should not be allowed to finance politics, but the same rules should apply to unions and other organizations. Only individuals should have these rights. To allow one set of special interests to play but not others cannot help cure the evils of crony capitalism. This is hard for many people who, like Bernie, have grown up with the myth that some special interests, in particular unions, are "good," while others are "evil," but this is not a factual or logical position.

> Long term, we need to go further and establish public funding of elections, so that the dark money of American politics is stopped before democracy is bought and paid for by a handful of billionaires and corporations.
>
> Des Moines, Iowa, June 12, 2015

The funding of political campaigns is a devilishly difficult subject. Should wealthy people be allowed to use their own money to run for office, when other candidates do not have the same resources? If forbidden by law, would that be a violation of the constitutional guarantee of free speech?

Is it desirable for candidates to be forced to seek many small gifts? Yes, so long as this does not lead to a proliferation of candidates financed by extremist groups, while most voters remain aloof. We must always consider possible unintended consequences.

What would happen if government funded all electioneering? Would this not let the fox into the hen house? When our only protection against crooked, corrupt, or ineffectual politicians is to remove them from office, what would prevent them from voting themselves massive campaign war chests. Who would stop them and how? Should we not expect public funding at least to favor incumbents, who unlike others would automatically become eligible.

Consider also what happened to public funding of presidential elections. In 2008, Republican candidate John McCain pledged to abide by the existing rules in order to earn the available public funding for his campaign. So, initially, did Barrack Obama. But when Obama realized that he could raise unprecedented sums, far more than McCain, he dropped out of public funding and in effect ended the program as a viable option for future candidates. From then on, out-fundraising your opponent became a principal means of winning the presidency.

In late spring and early summer of 2012, when President Obama, unopposed within his own party, had plenty of money, he invested in a massive advertising campaign designed to portray his opponent, Mitt Romney, as a heartless capitalist who had amassed a vast fortune by gutting companies and pitilessly destroying workers' jobs.

None of this had any resemblance to the facts. But Romney later claimed that at this moment he had exhausted his funds running in primaries against Republican opponents, and lacked the money to respond.

Romney's predicament also seems to have affected his campaign in other ways. In his nomination acceptance speech and elsewhere in his campaign, he seemed to concentrate on rebutting earlier Obama ads by presenting himself as a nice person whom ordinary people should not reject on moral or character grounds. This meant that he largely held his fire in attacking his opponent's policies. President Obama's Democratic strategists later claimed that the early ads portraying Romney as an evil capitalist greatly contributed to Obama's reelection in the fall.

There is much, much more to say about the role of the rich in the economy and in politics, but we will save it for the next chapter.

7

More on the Role
of the Rich*

THE OVERALL EQUALITARIAN case against the rich, not just Bernie's specific version of it, and the rebuttal of that argument may be summarized as a series of arguments:

Argument 1 against the Rich: The rich are essentially parasites. Wealth causes poverty; without rich people there would be no poor people.

Political commentator George Will thinks this argument absurd: "People are not hungry in Bombay [now Mumbai] because people are well-fed in Boston."[1].

---

* The following is a revised and condensed version of text from chapters 4, 5, and 7 from the author's book *Are The Rich Necessary? Great Economic Arguments and How They Reflect Our Personal Values, Updated & Expanded Edition* (Mt. Jackson, VA: Axios Press, 2009).

But it is undeniable that desperately poor people need more money, and others are awash in money.

If the top one percent of American earners gave away half their net income after tax to charity, and those funds went directly to the American poor, poverty as defined by the government would be eliminated. On the other hand, these same funds spread globally would barely dent the problem.

Argument 2 against the Rich: Very rich people steal from or exploit the poor.

As early French socialist P. J. Proudhon said in 1840, "property is theft."[2]

Monsignor Alfonso Lopez Trujillo, Secretary General of the Latin American Bishops' Conference, has written that "the United States and Canada are rich because the peoples of Latin America are poor. They have built their wealth on top of us."[3]

Julius Nyerere, long-time president of Tanzania and respected leader of the "Third World" during the US-Soviet Cold War, said that "when I am rich because you are poor . . . the transfer of wealth from the rich to the poor is a matter of right. It is not an appropriate matter of charity."[4]

Ronald J. Sider, equalitarian author of *Rich Christians in an Age of Hunger*, agrees with Nyerere's diagnosis, but thinks a better answer would be for the West to "lead a simpler, less extravagant lifestyle."[5]

The equalitarian case against rich people is compelling. Questions of exploitation aside, why would the rich not share what they have with the poor?

Counter-Argument 1: Our economy needs rich people precisely because they are rich.

The basic idea is as follows. Everyone—rich, middle class, or poor—benefits from an expanding economy. An economy expands by becoming more productive. We become more productive by learning how to produce more and more, better and better, with the same number of workers. Productivity increases as we give workers better tools. In order to afford these tools, we need to put away some of what we make each year. That is, we need to save, so that we can invest the savings in the tools we need.

The problem then arises: how to induce people to save? The poor cannot be expected to save, because they need every dollar for basic needs such as food and shelter. Middle class people will save something for emergencies, children's education, or old age. But they have many immediate needs and desires, and in any case their savings will eventually be consumed, especially after retirement. The rich, however, are different. They have so much money that, in aggregate, they simply cannot spend it all. They are, in effect, forced to save.

As economist Wilhelm Röpke has explained,

> the notion of the rich gluttonously stuffing them-
> selves is inexact, the stomach capacity of most in-
> dividuals being approximately the same. Of course,
> the larger . . . a [person's] income, the greater will
> be [the] consumption of luxury goods. . . . But even
> such luxury wants [cannot] absorb the whole of a
> very large income. The result is that the unspent por-
> tion of the very large income is saved.[6]

Of course, one can decide that the state will take over
the saving and investment function by taxing away the
rich person's wealth. But the problem quickly arises that
the state, unlike rich people, never runs out of things
to spend money on. Moreover, public officials are like
other people: they prefer to spend rather than save, and
there is no way to compel governments to become sav-
ers, since governments by definition control the social
instruments of compulsion. In the case of the Soviet
Union, the government chose to spend larger and larger
sums on weapons, and that money could not simultaneously be used for productive investment.

Just how important is savings and investment? In
the first place, it is precisely the failure to save and
invest, and to protect savings, that has kept humanity
so poor. In the second place, it may be argued that our
very lives depend on the steady increase in our capital.
As economic writer Henry Hazlitt has pointed out,

> aside from the notorious fact that the condition of
> the masses is enormously better than it was . . . before

the Industrial Revolution . . . , there is the still more notorious fact that the population of the world since then has increased [many-fold]. It was capital accumulation that made this possible. This means that . . . [many] of us owe our very existence to the savings and investments of our forebears.[7]

Counter-Argument 2: There cannot be too much saving if it is invested properly.

Some economists have responded that the rich save too much and spend too little, that jobs would be more plentiful and everyone would be better off if money came out from under mattresses and circulated more freely. This would be true if the rich really kept their money hidden in mattresses. But the lure of earning interest or capital gains usually ensures that money circulates whether it is spent or saved. If a rich person buys a yacht, this creates jobs for yacht-makers. But if, instead, the rich person buys some shares of stock from a company, and the company then uses the money to build a plant, there will also be more jobs for plant construction workers.

In terms of immediate new jobs created, spending and investment are equivalent. But there the similarity stops because investment spurs productivity, which leads to economic growth, which creates new jobs for the future.

Henry Hazlitt again:

Contrary to age-old prejudices, the wealth of the rich is not the cause of the poverty of the poor, but helps to alleviate that poverty. No matter whether it is their intention or not, almost anything that the rich can legally do tends to help the poor. The spending of the rich gives employment to the poor. But the saving of the rich, and their investment of these savings in the means of production, gives just as much employment, and in addition makes that employment constantly more productive and more highly paid, while it also constantly increases and cheapens the production of necessities and amenities for the masses.[8]

The rich should of course be directly charitable in the conventional sense to people who because of illness, disability or other misfortune cannot take employment or earn enough. Conventional forms of private charity should constantly be extended. But . . . those who truly want to help the poor will not spend their days in organizing protest marches.[9]

The most effective way for the rich to help the poor is to live simply, to avoid extravagance and ostentatious display, to save and invest so as to provide more people with increasingly productive jobs, and to provide the masses with an ever-greater abundance of the necessities and amenities of life.[10]

Everything Hazlitt wrote must be tempered somewhat by the realization that crony capitalism does not work this way. Rich crony capitalists live off government, do not serve the needs of consumers, do not live simply, and do not make economically useful investments. They are indeed parasites, just as both Marx and Bernie think they are.

Counter-Argument 3: The rich have a job to do, and if they shirk it or do it badly, they will likely lose their money.

Hazlitt expects what might be called the legitimate rich not only to save and invest, but to invest wisely. This can sometimes be accomplished by hiring others to make decisions, but however it is done, the results are what count. If the present guardians of social savings invest well, as measured by business profits and economic growth, they deserve to stay rich or become even richer. If they invest poorly, the system will quickly take their savings away, as it should.

The problem of quality, as opposed to quantity, of investment lies at the heart of economics. But it has received surprisingly little attention from modern economists. Only a rare text focuses on the importance of making sound investments, even though quality matters much more than quantity of investment in producing economic growth.

It is ultimately consumers who decide if an investment has been socially useful. If they find the product or service to be valuable and sold at a reasonable price, they will buy, and the investor has the chance to become rich. Government too can make investments, but by definition these investments are politicized and also hampered by lack of expertise, business experience, and a time horizon that seldom extends beyond the next election.

That consumers are the ultimate bosses in a genuine market economy (as opposed to a crony capitalist one) has been articulated by economist Ludwig von Mises:

> Descriptive terms which people use are often quite misleading. In talking about modern captains of industry and leaders of big business, for instance, they call a man a "chocolate king" or a "cotton king" or an "automobile king." Their use of such terminology implies that they see practically no difference between the modern heads of industry and those feudal kings, dukes or lords of earlier days. But the difference is in fact very great, for a chocolate king does not rule at all, he serves. This "king" must stay in the good graces of his subjects, the consumers; he loses his "kingdom" as soon as he is no longer in a position to give his customers better service and provide it at lower cost than others with whom he must compete.[11]

The acid test for any productive system of economic inequality is that there must be downward as well as upward mobility for the rich, that the consumer must be able to give, but also to take away.

The evidence of downward mobility for companies clearly exists, but what about for rich people? Here we have at least the following:

- The US Internal Revenue Service reports that over a nine-year-period only 1% of the names on the list of the 400 highest-paying taxpayers remained the same every year.[12]

- *Forbes* magazine reports that over a twenty-two-year period only 50 individuals or 13% of its list of the 400 richest Americans (assets, not income) managed to stay on the list for the full period.[13]

- Glenn Hubbard, a Treasury Department official and later chairman of the President's Council of Economic Advisors, looked at the top 1% of US taxpayers at the start and end of a ten-year period, and found that over a third fell out of the top group and that the initial top group's average income fell by 11%.[14]

Counter-Argument 4: The charge that the rich can only make others better off through a "trickle-down" process is false.

Equalitarians often mock their opponents for espousing a "trickle-down" theory of economics, one that wants to make the rich richer as the first step in making others richer. Economist Thomas Sowell disagrees and regards the very concept of "trickle down" as erroneous. As he says,

> it is nonsense to [describe economic growth as] "trickling down" [from the rich]. . . . The [rich person's] investment has to happen first, and workers have to be hired and paid first, before the investor has any hope of reaping any gains. Since capital gains come last, not first, they do not "trickle down."[15]

Counter-Argument 5: What would actually happen if the government decided to seize rich people's assets entirely in order to give them to the poor?

The rich hold most of their wealth in the form of bonds, stocks, or real estate, all of which rise and fall in price depending on market demand for them. If word spread that wealth would be redistributed, buyers of these assets would disappear and prices plummet. Later, after assets were seized, they would have to be sold in order to provide cash to distribute. But the lack of buyers would make the sales impossible.

Meanwhile, companies, unsure of the future flow of savings, would stop investing, with the result that many people would lose their jobs. In effect, then, the great risk of all redistribution schemes, however well intentioned, is that savings and investment, that is, the capital underlying the economy, are simply destroyed. Even if the rich voluntarily decided to sell their assets in order to distribute cash to the poor, the same sequence of events would unfold.

8

Bernie for Equality

Unbelievably, and grotesquely, the top one-tenth
of 1 percent owns nearly as much wealth as the
bottom 90 percent.

On Democratic Socialism in the United States,
November 19, 2015

We are living at a time where a handful of people
have wealth beyond comprehension—huge yachts,
jet planes, tens of billions of dollars, more money
that they could spend in a thousand life-times, while,
at the same time, millions of people are struggling
to feed their families or put a roof over their heads
or find the money to go to a doctor.

Liberty University Convocation,
September 14, 2015

MOST AMERICANS ARE uncomfortable with
such extremes and would like to reduce them.
But how? To what degree do the extremes

reflect real market capitalism with its emphasis on free rather than controlled prices versus an economy severely distorted and corrupted by crony capitalism, with vast fortunes made from government favors and connections, and with the wheels of commerce jammed by government price controls and manipulations that are traded for campaign contributions and other favors.

As we have already noted, if the problem is crony capitalism, which involves a conspiracy of government with special interests against the public, then Bernie's proposed solution of giving the government even more money and power will not work. Indeed it is bound to make everything worse.

Crony capitalists deliberately make this as confusing as possible. In a May 16, 2014 speech on the economy, Hillary Clinton stated that "as secretary of state I saw the way extreme inequality corrupted other societies." This is a clever reversal of cause and effect. It is corruption, in particular crony capitalist corruption, that commonly creates the worst kind of inequality, in which the poor, the young, and the middle class fall further and further behind while rich government cronies thrive.

Back to Bernie:

> Today, one family, the Walton family of Walmart, owns more wealth than the bottom 130 million Americans!
>
> AFL-CIO Conference, August 18, 2015

This is certainly an unsettling statistic, and there are other reasons to be concerned about Walmart. Many rural small town main streets have fallen into irreversible decay because their customers drive up to an hour away to shop at Walmart.

> The issue of wealth and income inequality is the great economic issue of our time, the great political issue of our time, and the great moral issue of our time.
>
> The Urgency of a Moral Economy: Reflections on the 25th Anniversary of Centesimus Annus, April 15, 2016

Even with the extreme inequality described above, is the wide gap in wealth the primary economic as well as moral issue? Or is it the presence of poverty in the midst of plenty and a dwindling middle class with even more dwindling prospects? Would Bernie be satisfied if everyone were reduced to the same poverty? Is not the task to lift up those below rather than level everyone?

> I am told time and time again by the rich and powerful, and the mainstream media that represent them, that we should be "practical," that we should accept the status quo.
>
> The Urgency of a Moral Economy: Reflections on the 25th Anniversary of Centesimus Annus, April 15, 2016

Bernie is right that the American establishment (including much of the mainstream press) has a stake in the status quo and reflects that. Journalists are all too often just cogs in the crony capitalist system. Newspapers, magazines, broadcast stations, and internet sites are too often bought and paid for by Big Food, Big Pharma, and other advertisers.

> I am told time and time again . . . that a truly moral economy is beyond our reach.
>
> The Urgency of a Moral Economy: Reflections on the 25th Anniversary of Centesimus Annus, April 15, 2016

Is Bernie right here also? What is a moral economy? Is it best defined by the degree of equality? Or is it rather one that helps everyone realize their potential and lifts everyone out of poverty?

> Nearly five decades later, [Martin Luther] King [Jr.'s] words on the subject [of inequality] still ring true. On March 10, 1968, just weeks before his death, he spoke to a union group in New York about what he called "the other America." He was preparing to launch a Poor People's Campaign whose premise was that issues of jobs and issues of [racial] justice were inextricably intertwined. . . . The problem was structural, King said: "This country has socialism for the rich, rugged individualism for the poor."
>
> Southern Christian Leadership Conference, July 25, 2015

The term "socialism for the rich" rings all too true. This too is an expression of the underlying problem of crony capitalism in America. Too many rich people amass large fortunes through government favors and connections. There is welfare for the rich in the form of deductions for jumbo mortgages and Social Security or Medicare payments that serve no purpose other than running up the federal debt. Does it really make sense to borrow from China in order to subsidize the rich? Why are both Democrats and Republicans refusing to do anything about this?

Bernie again:

> This grotesque level of inequality is immoral. It is bad economics. It is unsustainable. That is why we need a tax system that is fair and progressive, which makes wealthy individuals and profitable corporations begin to pay their fair share of taxes.

> Des Moines, Iowa,
> June 12, 2015

Is this logical? If inequality is the central problem, why are much heavier government taxes the answer? This just transfers capital from investors who might use it to create businesses employing the poor and middle class and puts it in the hands of government bureaucrats who do not know the first thing about investing and who only deploy the word "investment" to cover up their own out-of-control deficit spending.

If we really want government mandated sharing of the wealth, then why not have government mandated charitable giving rather than confiscatory taxes? This could be accomplished easily enough. We could simply legislate that taxpayers in the highest brackets have the option to give to charity what they would otherwise have to pay in high bracket taxes.

Most rich people would prefer charitable giving to paying taxes, and many of them would become charitable investors seeking to get the most from their gifts. There would be a renaissance of charitable entrepreneurship and leadership. We would not only be putting money to work to solve social ills; we would be putting brains to work as well.

Bernie again:

> It is not acceptable that billionaire families are able to leave virtually all of their wealth to their families without paying a reasonable estate tax.
>
> On Democratic Socialism in the United States,
> November 19, 2015

As mentioned earlier, wealth taxes are especially damaging for an economy. They not only strip capital from existing or potential investors and entrepreneurs. They also require that businesses and farms and other property be sold for cash to feed into the maw of government. The scale of these sales would simply destroy asset markets.

All taxes create a drag on economic growth, but wealth taxes are especially destructive. Even John Maynard Keynes, the most influential progressive economist, argued against wealth taxes for this reason in the earlier years of his career, although he became more willing to consider them later.

We also need to keep in mind that wealth taxes are not limited estate or death taxes. Property taxes may also force sales of assets, especially among the poor or elderly. And some economists, most notably Thomas Piketty of France, have recommended very large wealth taxes.

9

More on Inequality*

THERE ARE MANY interesting arguments both for and against having a goal of economic equality. Even equalitarians differ in their viewpoint. As we shall see below, Bernie is a certain kind of economic equalitarian. For example, he does not endorse the kind of economic equalitarianism presented in Argument 1 below, but may have some personal sympathies for it.

Argument 1 for Equality: Living with others on a share-and-share-alike basis is the best way to live.

The proposal here is not necessarily one of state control of the economy. That was attempted in Russia and elsewhere during the twentieth century and was not a success.

---

* The following is a revised and condensed version of text from chapters 11 and 12 from the author's book *Are The Rich Necessary? Great Economic Arguments and How They Reflect Our Personal Values, Updated & Expanded Edition* (Mt. Jackson, VA: Axios Press, 2009).

❖ 75

The Israeli kibbutz provides a better example. Kibbutz members join together voluntarily and share everything as completely as possible on principle. In the early days before the formation of the State of Israel, this shared life was very hard. Malaria and dysentery had to be overcome, along with the harshest privations: cloth sacks stitched together for clothing, primitive communal privies, endless manual labor, three glasses to be shared by an entire community. All of this is vividly described by former Prime Minister Golda Meir in her memoirs. Today life is easier, but the ideal of a shared life remains.

An important manual of small-scale equalitarianism in Britain, America, India, and elsewhere is economist E. F. Schumacher's inspiring little book *Small is Beautiful*. Schumacher thought that the greatest obstacle to human peace and happiness is not institutional arrangements per se, but the "greed, envy, hate, and lust"[16] within all of us, and that large disparities of wealth inflame both greed and envy.

Spirituality, peacefulness, even pacifism are ever-present threads in the fabric of contemporary small-scale equalitarianism. President Luiz Inácio ("Lula") da Silva of Brazil spoke for most equalitarians when he told a meeting of the Socialist International in 2003 that "The only war we should be waging is against hunger and inequality. That's a war worth fighting."[17]

In addition to spirituality, non-materialism, and pacifism, ecology and environmental protection have also emerged as important themes of most small-scale equalitarian thinking. Thus the website of Twin Oaks, an intentional community of about eighty people near Charlottesville, Virginia, states that

> since the community's beginning in 1967, our way of life has reflected our values of cooperation, sharing, nonviolence, equality, and ecology.

All of this is in the most marked contrast to the old, Marxist, large-scale equalitarian ideology of the past, which specifically attacked spirituality and non-materialism, rationalized violence and aggression, and left the most horrendous environmental depredations.

Counter-Argument: Small-scale equalitarianism is a vast improvement over the large-scale, state-run version.

State-run equalitarianism is really a contradiction in terms. If sharing is a matter of law, it must be enforced. To be enforced, some individuals must be entrusted with police powers. If some people have police powers and others do not, how is that equal? It is simply an inequality of power rather than of money, and will soon mutate into an inequality of money as well, as it did in Communist Russia.

This is why the French Revolutionary slogan "liberty, equality, fraternity" is nonsensical. Liberty and equality are logical opposites. If people have liberty, they will become unequal. Even if government denies liberty to safeguard equality, equality will not last.

Small-scale equalitarianism is not illogical in the way that large-scale, state-run equalitarianism is. But there are reasons to doubt its practicality. The ancient Greek philosopher Aristotle pointed out that a share-and-share-alike approach to cooperation generally leads to conflict, because members of the group will not all work as hard, or will have sincere differences about the balance of work and leisure, either of which may lead to quarrels. From this point of view, an approach to cooperation that emphasizes independence, self-reliance, and reciprocal exchange will ultimately produce more friendship and mutual assistance.

In addition, if people are going to be quarrelsome about work or possessions, it is surely better to channel this aggression into prescribed forms of mutual exchange-based competition. As Samuel Johnson said, "There are few ways in which a man can be more innocently employed than in getting money."[18]

John Maynard Keynes made the same point:

> Dangerous human proclivities can be canalized into comparatively harmless channels by the opportunities for money-making and private wealth, which, if they cannot be satisfied in this way, may find their outlet in cruelty, the reckless pursuit of personal power and authority, and other forms of self-aggrandizement. It

> is better that a man should tyrannize over his bank
> balance than over his fellow-citizens.[19]

Some opponents of equalitarianism regard all its associated tenets as hopelessly utopian, especially its pacifism. Here is what Joseph Alsop, leading political columnist after World War II, said about it:

> What do we need in America to endure? Every-
> body else [in the world] would like to divide up our
> goods. They'd like to chew us up like a dead whale
> on a beach, if we'd let them do it. And I have the
> warmest sympathy for that desire. It is perfectly un-
> derstandable, and we mustn't complain about it.[20]

Argument 2 for Equality: Income inequality, especially extreme inequality, is both unjust and uncharitable. Only government action can at least improve the situation. (This is Bernie's view.)

On the one hand, billions of people desperately lack money for the barest necessities. On the other hand, a lucky individual may be fêted and showered with money just because he can dribble or throw a ball a bit better than others, or because he or she was born to rich parents. Between the extremes, we have dedicated and talented teachers and social workers who are woefully, even scandalously, underpaid.

This system, as John Maynard Keynes said, is both "arbitrary and inequitable." Even if some degree of inequality is desirable for motivational purposes, as Keynes further observed: "Much lower stakes will serve the purpose equally well."[21]

The winners under this system should ask themselves: do I really deserve to have all this when others have so little? And, have I really "earned" it? Even if I have worked hard and made prudent choices, how far would I have gotten without the support of others?

Counter-Argument: Our personal incomes are in no sense arbitrary. They are determined by supply and demand.

Supply and demand tell us, in unequivocal terms, how useful we are in the eyes of others. Norman Van Cott explains:

> Our incomes—be they large, small or somewhere in between—reflect (1) our usefulness to our fellow citizens and (2) the ease with which fellow citizens can find substitutes for us.[22]

We may not want to hear the market's message. But the market does not discriminate. Only people discriminate. Employers who do so become less efficient, lose good employees or customers, suffer higher costs, and thus pay a penalty of lower profits. Over time, markets eradicate discrimination by persuading bigoted employers that they cannot afford to indulge their prejudices.

We may understandably object that markets treat people too much like commodities. But our labor (as distinct from ourselves) is a commodity, and is priced by consumers in exactly the same understandable and consistent way that other commodities are priced. There is nothing inequitable about this.

It may be objected that our financial success depends, not simply on effort or merit, but to a large extent on luck. If so, we are not lucky or unlucky in money alone. We are all lucky to become fetuses, since the odds are infinitesimal that any particular two gene pools will ever merge, we are lucky to be born, and lucky to reach maturity. From there we are lucky or unlucky in the genes we get, the brains, looks, personality, talents, parents, education, health, neighborhood, country, or times in which we live.

If equality is synonymous with justice, we live in a hopelessly unjust world. Are we going to try to level all these playing fields? And if so, how, and who will decide what is level? As economist Thomas Sowell has observed:

> The difference between a factory worker and an executive is nothing compared to the difference between being born brain-damaged and being born normal, or the difference between being born to loving parents rather than abusive parents.[23]

If we are going to try to do something about this, we will first have to figure out how to measure the degree of brain damage or parental abuse. Then we will need to arrive at a reasonable compensation formula. Will we also try to provide equally good parents or equally good teachers for every child? Will we demand that leading universities agree to teach any child who applies, and what will we do when we run out of these universities assuming that we can still regard them as leading universities?

Later in life, will we follow the now old people into their doctor's office to be sure that they all get exactly the same pill for the same malady, assuming that it is the same malady? If these examples seem far-fetched, it should be noted that contemporary philosophers have debated similar issues, because they do help us define what exactly we mean by equalitarianism.

Argument 3 for Equality:

Yes, inequality is deeply imbedded in all life as we know it. But that is not a reason to abandon economic equality; it is all the more reason to pursue it. If life is inherently unequal, then let us make equal what we can, especially the economy, since that is the work of our own hands.

Counter-Argument:

It is a mirage to think that economic equality is easier to achieve than other kinds of equality. If you give two individuals exactly the same income, one may save, invest, and grow rich, while the other may sink into torpor or debt. What is to be done then? Should we re-equalize the situation? How will that be done and how often? If we keep re-equalizing, will the saving and investing individual go on doing so? The evidence of history is that when government does not protect private property, but even preys on it, investment stops, and the economy collapses.

There are additional complexities. To promote equality, one must be consistent, because inconsistent outcomes cannot be equal. But equalitarians are necessarily inconsistent. They may prescribe heavy taxation on all incomes over X, which might be an average or a "middle-class" income of people in their own country. But, in doing so, they ignore the fact that a fifth of humanity is living on less than $1 a day.[24]

If redistributive policies are to be followed, should we not apply them worldwide? Bernie is very much guilty of this inconsistency. And he doubles down on it by saying that although we should not export our jobs to other countries, and thus impoverish our workers, we should open our borders to mass immigration of the poor, which will produce tremendous new competition for our workers and drive their wages down.

Consistency is one logical principle; clarity and completeness are others. To their critics, equalitarian arguments are unclear and incomplete, as well as inconsistent, because they fail to distinguish between unequal outcomes that change over time and unequal outcomes that are simply frozen. In traditional societies, inequality exists because of the lack of social mobility, that is, because positions are largely frozen. Free-market competition may increase economic inequality, but also social mobility. Winners and losers change. Moreover, the social mobility implicit in free-market competition tends to reduce inequality over time, not increase it. Economist Milton Friedman has observed that

> the development of [free markets] has greatly lessened the extent of inequality. . . . [25] Nowhere is the gap between rich and poor wider, nowhere are the rich richer and the poor poorer, than in those countries that do not permit the free market to operate.[26]

It should be readily apparent that economic equality, the equality of result, is incompatible with equality of opportunity. Most honest people will see advantages to both. But we must choose. We cannot have both, and if we have more of one we must accept less of the other.

Argument 4 for Equality:

Milton Friedman's assertion is nonsense. As Jeffrey Gates, head of the Shared Capitalism Institute, has said, "Capitalism does not raise all boats; it raises all yachts."[27]

Counter-Argument:

Economist Steve H. Hanke responds to Jeffrey Gates by citing a World Bank study by David Dollar and Aart Kraay. This study looked at eighty countries over four decades and concluded that free markets help "the poor" at least as much as the "non-poor." In addition, Dollar and Kraay found that the poor are especially benefited by controlling inflation and also by controlling the growth of government spending. Why government spending? As Hanke puts it, "The rich are much better placed to feed at the public trough. The poor get crumbs."[28]

We might also recall that, precisely because money means more to the poor than the rich, a rise in incomes through economic growth helps the poor disproportionately. As Henry Hazlitt reminds us,

> the overwhelming majority of Americans . . . now enjoy the advantages of running water, central heating, telephones, automobiles, refrigerators, washing machines, [electronic music,] radios, television sets—amenities that millionaires and kings did not enjoy a few generations ago.[29]

Indeed, a study by the Heritage Foundation found that 41% of the official poor in the United States owned their own home. A majority owned automobiles as well as microwaves, DVD players, and air conditioning.

Argument 5 for Equality:

Even if it were true that equalitarian policies slowed economic growth, with possible negative impact on the prospects for the poor, would that invalidate the idea of sharing at least some of the wealth more equally now? Economist Arthur Okun, a former chairman of the President's Council of Economic Advisors, said that "I would prefer . . . complete [economic] equality."[30] But he has also suggested that trading off some "growth" for some "equity" is a reasonable compromise.

Counter-Argument:

Equalitarians like to think of the economy as a machine with bells, whistles, and levers, all of which can be manipulated to produce more of this or less of that. But this is an illusion. As thinker and writer Irving Kristol has observed, "If you want economic growth, only that species of activity called 'business' can get it for you. The 'economy,' as conventionally understood, cannot."[31]

What this means is that, to have more economic growth, you must support businessmen or women, and demotivating them or reducing the savings available to them through income redistribution schemes will not help. Moreover, once you start down this path, intending to go only a short distance, it is often very hard to stop, for reasons explained by economist Sanford Ikeda: "Redistributional policies . . . typically aggravate the . . . problems . . . thereby providing even greater justification for more intervention."[32]

Argument 6 for Equality:

Income and wealth inequality is increasing at an alarming rate in the United States, as confirmed by a succession of studies. The 1994 *Economic Report of the President*, written by the President's Council of Economic Advisors, drew upon some of the earlier studies to state unequivocally that "Starting sometime in the late 1970s, income inequalities widened alarmingly in America."[33] Since then, and especially since the mid-1990s, it has increased even more rapidly. Is society, acting through government, to stand back and do nothing about this?

Counter-Argument:

The emergence of a truly global economy has reduced global inequality by increasing incomes in developing countries. At the same time, it has left lower-paid workers in developed countries struggling. Crony capitalist policies pursued by world governments have made all this worse, much worse.

Unfortunately none of this can be measured accurately. Since the Clinton administration, US and world government efforts to doctor economic data have become ever more blatant, and even before then the data were not very intelligently or carefully collected.

For example, government personal income data is distorted because many businesses report on personal rather than corporate income tax return forms and this trend is sharply increasing, primarily because of the growing use of Limited Liability Companies (LLCs) as the favored form of business organization. When income that used to be reported on corporate returns as corporate income is shifted to personal returns, it can seem that high-end incomes are growing more rapidly than they really are.

Government income data is also not reported per individual, but rather per "household." The problem here is that "households" may include zero, one, two or more wage earners. This makes comparison misleading. Moreover, household size changes a great deal over time. In particular, poor "households" have fewer members today than in the past, which may partly explain why they are poor.

Age too is very important: the same individual may be counted as poor when a student, rich in middle age, and poor again in old age, so changes in the average age of the population skew results. Immigration also matters, although it is rarely considered in income inequality statistics. Immigrants, especially in the US, tend to start out as very poor and this can distort what is happening in the bottom decile or quintile.

The way income is defined matters a great deal. Government statistics vary considerably in what they include or exclude, and the decisions often make no sense. For example, transfer payments such as the earned income tax credit, welfare payments, and social security income are not counted. One of the worst mistakes is treating a capital gain as personal income. When people sell a stock, receive cash, and realize a capital gain (that is, sell an asset for more than it cost), they actually exchange one asset for another rather than create economic income. It would also help to know how many hours people work for their income. If person A works 40 hours and person B works 80 hours, most people would not think it unequal for B to be paid twice as much.

In any case, none of the available US government statistics exclude business income and provide reliable per capita (per person), age-adjusted, immigration-adjusted, work-hour-adjusted, income-definition-adjusted data. Without this information, it is almost certain that income inequality has been increasing in the United States, in large part driven by the government's own crony capitalist policies, but it cannot be accurately measured.

Part Four

Corporate America and Trade

10

Bernie against Corporate Greed

Corporate greed is destroying this country and, whether [companies] like it or not, that greed and destructiveness is going to end.

New Hampshire Democratic Party Convention,
September 19, 2015

Much of the corporate [owned or controlled] media is prepared to discuss everything except the most important issues facing our country.

Southern Christian Leadership Conference, July 25,
2015

The greed of United Technologies is almost unbelievable. You can't make this stuff up. They have no shame.

This is a company that in 2014 provided its retired CEO, Louis Schenevert, with a golden parachute of $172 million—including a pension worth $31 million.

And they apparently got rid of him because he was doing a bad job! Imagine what they would have given him if he was doing a good job. . . .

This is a company that received $6 billion in defense contracts last year from the taxpayers of this country.

. . . This is a company that has received more than $58 million in corporate welfare from the Export-Import Bank. That is unacceptable.

This is a company that in 2009 received $121 million in federal tax credits designed specifically to keep green manufacturing jobs in the United States.

United Steelworkers Rally, April 29, 2016

THERE IS SOMETHING missing from Bernie's otherwise accurate account here. If this company received more than $58 million in corporate welfare and $121 million in federal tax credits, is it not primarily an indictment of our government? Can we really expect corporations not to fatten at the trough if government keeps it full of feed? What is really being described here is not corporate greed but rather our crony capitalist system.

The pay scale of CEOs of public companies was once a private matter. During the Clinton administration, government began regulating it, and the regulations have totally backfired, as they usually do when government imposes price controls in any market, including the market for CEOs.

Bernie again:

> It makes no sense that large profitable corporations like Pfizer think they can leave this country and become foreign companies to avoid paying their fair share of taxes, while they continue charging us the highest prices in the world for prescription drugs.
>
> New Hampshire Democratic Party
> Jefferson-Jackson Dinner, November 29, 2015

Again this is leaving out much of the story. Why are US drug prices so high? The drugs themselves often cost only pennies per tablet to make. The reason that drug companies can charge so much is that they enjoy government granted monopolies.

Here is how it works. To take a new drug through the Food and Drug Administration (FDA) approval process costs billions of dollars on average. Consequently, companies will only undertake this expense for patented substances. Patenting a substance provides one government protected monopoly. FDA approval provides a second layer of government enforced monopoly protection, because the approval is exclusive to one drug and even one use of the drug. It does not cover drugs of the same class, each one of which must also seek approval at vast expense.

Natural substances, which may be far less toxic and more effective, are simply shut out of the system. Being natural they cannot be patented, so companies will not submit them for approval. Not being approved, doctors are afraid to use them. They fear losing their medical licenses for doing so.

Drug companies themselves understand that natural substances are on average safer and often very effective. They may start with a natural substance, then twist the molecules so that it becomes a new-to-nature product. Unfortunately being new to nature, it may be quite toxic, because our bodies do not recognize it and have not had a chance to co-evolve with it.

Trials may indicate that it is safe, or at least does not exhibit too many side effects. But more and more toxic drugs are being approved, and just reading the drug insert about possible side effects can be terrifying. Drug companies rely on consumers not to read their inserts but just take whatever their doctors give them, which given today's crony capitalist medicine is foolish behavior. Patients need to do some research, which is readily available on the internet, and protect themselves. No one else will.

Drug trials do not usually include the very young and the very old, and it is the old who more often get the drugs. Often it is only after approval and after millions of people have taken the drug that it becomes apparent how dangerous it really is. The classic example of this is the painkiller Vioxx®, which is believed to have killed people by leading to heart disease or cancer, but there are numerous examples.

Many commonly used drugs such as acid blockers and statins have very dangerous side effects. Drug companies have made billions on them, but in the end will probably have to give some of it back in class action legal settlements or judgements. The people whose health has been wrecked will not of course be made whole by any of these after-the-fact payments.

Finally, the government, which has created these drug monopolies, and benefits directly from them in the form of both campaign contributions and payments to the FDA, has outlawed the importation of drugs from abroad. The drugs available in Canadian and other pharmacies may have been made by the same US manufacturer, so are identical to the US product, but typically sell for a fraction of the US price, because of foreign government price controls. The US government claims to outlaw foreign imports for quality assurance reasons, but this is a smokescreen. It is really just doing the bidding of the drug companies and protecting their government granted monopolies.

Bernie probably favors allowing the import of foreign drugs, but he says nothing about the larger problems of medical crony capitalism, and the government's complicity in it.

Bernie again:

> Social Security, the minimum wage, Medicare and Medicaid, affordable housing . . . Today, all of those accomplishments are under attack by some of

> the wealthiest people and largest corporations
> in this country.
>
> AFL-CIO Conference, August 18, 2015

Bernie does not document these charges. Which large corporation does he think is trying to repeal all these programs? Big companies are very comfortable with the crony capitalist system. All the government regulation tends to protect them from competition from newer and smaller and more innovative companies. They are not likely to risk offending either the government or many of their customers by taking on Social Security, minimum wage, Medicare and Medicaid, or housing programs.

> Brothers and sisters, . . . You have seen CEOs earn
> 300 times what their average workers make. You have
> seen workers fired for standing up for their rights to
> collectively bargain. You have seen the transformation
> of our country away from a General Motors econ-
> omy of good wages and good benefits to a Walmart
> economy of starvation wages and no benefits.
>
> AFL-CIO Conference, August 18, 2015

Bernie should document the assertion that workers are being fired for supporting unionization, since it would be illegal to do so. We have already discussed in a previous chapter how the unions destroyed General Motors and then ended up owning it thanks to some illegal actions by the Obama Administration.

Good wages and good benefits cannot be ordered by government. In order to achieve them, companies and workers must cooperate to produce the best possible goods and services at the lowest possible price. In our crony capitalist world, with ceaseless government price controls and manipulations, and with access to government the best way to get rich, it is increasingly difficult to produce either honest profits or the good wages that flow from them.

Bernie again:

> In 2007 I heard about horrendous [undocumented worker] exploitation in Immokalee, Florida. . . . On the day that I arrived . . . there . . . , amazingly enough, the US Attorney . . . was indicting some people on slavery, people being held in slavery, forced to work against their will. I saw the conditions of workers working horrendously long hours at very low wages, very bad working conditions, awful housing and I'm happy to say that with people working together we made some progress. Today workers there get better wages, get better working conditions and better housing.
>
> National Council of La Raza, August 12, 2015

Slavery is illegal, as it should be. So is both hiring and exploitation of what Bernie calls undocumented workers, which is a euphemism for illegal immigrants. When government sets out rules for the economy, and acts as an umpire in the interpretation and enforcement of the rules, it is playing a proper role. When, in sharp contrast, it starts controlling and manipulating prices, exchanging favors with favored companies, or otherwise trying to run the economy itself, it makes the kind of mess we are seeing today.

11

More on the Profit System[*]

BERNIE IS A self-described socialist and socialists generally reject the profit system. When Bernie labels most companies as "greedy," it is not clear whether he is rejecting the profit system itself or just how these particular companies conduct themselves. Perhaps there is not much distinction in his mind.

Bernie favors "Medicare for all" and thus would concentrate virtually all of healthcare in government hands. But government already pays for at least half of healthcare and closely regulates the rest. Moreover the federal government does not actually operate Medicare. That is farmed out to private companies.

---

[*] The following is a revised and condensed version of text from chapters 8 and 9 from the author's book *Are The Rich Necessary? Great Economic Arguments and How They Reflect Our Personal Values, Updated & Expanded Edition* (Mt. Jackson, VA: Axios Press, 2009).

All of this seems to favor a "corporatist" model, one in which government controls the economy but does not directly own it. Bernie explicitly says that he does not want government to abolish private property or claim nominal ownership of everything as in the former Soviet Union. It is important to note, however, that this "corporatist" model is not a genuine market system. Government not only regulates even minute details of the economy. It also controls or manipulates prices, and through prices, profits as well. With controlled or manipulated prices, it is neither a free price system nor a true profit system.

As we have noted, all of this is a recipe for more and more cronyism. Businesses come to realize that the road to profit lies through Washington, not through meeting the needs of consumers in honest competition with other producers. Other special interests clamor for benefits and favors for themselves in return for campaign contributions and other pay-offs to all powerful public officials.

These are complicated matters, not very well captured by slogans. In order to make sense of them, we need to take the time to step back and consider the arguments both against and for a genuine "free market" price and profit system, not a phony or crony version of it. Through the arguments, we will also better understand what such a system is and is not. We will begin with the question of whether the profit system is efficient.

Argument 1 against the Profit System: By definition it must be inefficient.

Profit is an unnecessary, extra cost piled on top of genuine production costs. As such, it is wasteful. If this waste were eliminated, prices would fall and everyone would be better off. As philosopher Ted Honderich has stated this case:

> If there are two ways of [producing] some valuable thing, and the second way involves not only the costs of [producing] it . . . but also [unnecessary] profits of millions or billions of dollars or pounds, then . . . the second way is patently and tremendously less efficient.[34]

Counter-Argument: Prices and profits work together as an indispensable signaling device.

The desire and need, that is, the demand for particular products is constantly shifting. People choose this now, that later. Meanwhile the supply of products also shifts depending on an infinite number of variables (for example, weather affects the supply of crops). Information about both demand and supply is communicated to everyone by prices. Higher prices signal more demand or less supply, lower prices signal the opposite. This radically simplifies economic life.

As important as prices are for signaling conditions, they cannot do their work without profits. For example, assume that I am in the applesauce business and that profits are high because of heavy consumer demand or unusually low apple or sugar costs. The high profits give me the cash (or the credit) to step up my production. In addition other producers will likely do the same, and some new producers may be attracted into the business. In either case, supply will rise until profits fall back to more modest levels.

On the other hand, if profits fall far enough, supply will contract, so that output will again be brought into better balance with consumer demand. Everybody who wants applesauce will then get it, and producers will earn the profits necessary to keep recreating a balance. The key point to remember is that the quest for profits in a competitive market tends to increase supply, thereby lower, not raise consumer prices. The quest for profits also drives competitors to work hard at lowering their costs. The dynamic of competition eventually translates lower costs into both higher wages and lower consumer prices.

The profit system is especially good at identifying "chokepoints" or "bottlenecks" in the economic system, places where production is difficult or inefficient and where profit "tolls" are consequently high. For example, Mark Kurlansky in his book *Cod* has sketched the development of the huge cod-fishing industry since the sixteenth century, an industry that in earlier centuries furnished a high percentage of the total protein available to Europeans. At first the choke-point was the ships, which were too small and flimsy. This attracted capital and better ship designs, so that the profit of ship owners eventually fell.

The next chokepoint was ports immediately adjacent to the fishing grounds, because the fish could not be kept long without processing, and nearby processors were able to charge high rates. As ships got faster, however, the small ports were bypassed, and the chokepoint moved to larger ports such as Boston. These larger ports were much more efficient than the smaller ones, but still commanded high prices and earned high profits. Finally, refrigerated container ships enabled fishing companies to bypass processing centers entirely.

Step by step, investment flowed to where the process was least efficient, where high profits signaled both a problem and an opportunity. In each case, the problems were solved, the chokepoint profits were reduced or eliminated through investment and competition, and consumers directly benefited from the increase in efficiency through steadily declining prices.[35] Although everyone benefited from this process, the poor benefited especially, because it meant that they could afford more protein in their diet.

Even Karl Marx, the father of Communism, acknowledged that the profit system reduces prices. He said as much in the *Communist Manifesto* of 1848:

> The cheap prices of its commodities are the heavy artillery with which [the profit system] . . . compels all

nations, on pain of extinction, to adopt the [profit] mode of production.[36]

When the Soviet Union came into being during World War I as the first Communist state, many of its founders assumed that both prices and profits would be abolished. This was complicated by Marx's puzzling failure to suggest exactly how this might be done. A decision was eventually reached to keep prices and profits, although the latter would be "for all."

Economist Ludwig von Mises responded that a system of public prices and profits was impossible, that only private prices and profits could provide the necessary information flow and calculations, and thus organize, direct, and grow an economy. Von Mises summarized the problem in this way:

> It is not enough to tell a man not to buy on the cheapest market and not to sell on the dearest market. . . . One must establish unambiguous rules for the guidance of conduct in each concrete situation.[37]

Von Mises's thesis was violently disputed but never successfully rebutted, either in theory or in practice. The Soviet Union by the 1960s had from five to nine price and profit systems according to varying accounts, but none seemed to work.[38] As Oystein Dahle, a Norwegian oil executive, has said, "Socialism collapsed because it did not allow prices to tell the economic truth."[39]

Profits are also indispensable as a system of positive and negative incentives that are objectively scored.

We usually think of the game of business being scored in profits, but it is even more importantly scored in losses and bankruptcies. As economist Wilhelm Röpke has written:

> Since the fear of loss appears to be of more moment than the desire for gain, it may be said that our economic system (in the final analysis) is regulated by bankruptcy.[40]

Economist Milton Friedman has similarly argued that the "profit" system should really be called the "profit and loss" system, that the "stick" is at least as important as the "carrot."

The carrot of profit and the stick of loss in general persuade us either to change or to accept change, something that people are more often than not reluctant to do. Economic growth by definition entails change; without it we would all still be hunting and gathering, or at least those few of us who could still survive within such a restricted economic environment. Yet many people are simply uncomfortable with change, others may be lazy, and vested interests will always fight hard against change if they can.

People can of course be motivated to change by other, more directly coercive methods. Stalin bent millions to his will through sheer terror. But, as a general rule, coercion is extremely inefficient, because people have a thousand ways of resisting, passively as well as actively. If one reads the memoirs of large slaveowners in the American South in the 1850s,[41] they fret about the ceaseless passive resistance of the slaves, even in the face of cruel punishments. That such an inefficient system survived at all can only be attributed to the boom prices being paid at the time for American cotton by English clothing manufacturers.

12

Other Critiques of the Profit System[*]

Argument 2 against the Profit System: This system pits owners and workers against each other in a ceaseless struggle, a struggle that is ultimately self-defeating for everyone.

Businesses may create profits by overcharging consumers. A more common tactic is to underpay employees. Labor unions have helped level the playing field, but only a bit.

Counter-Argument: It is understandable but very mistaken to think that profits are "stolen" from workers.

Do not workers' wages come out of the "skin" of owners and vice versa? Is this not a classic example of a "zero-sum game"? Actually, no, it is not.

---

[*] The following is a revised and condensed version of text from chapters 8, 9, and 10 from the author's book *Are The Rich Necessary? Great Economic Arguments and How They Reflect Our Personal Values, Updated & Expanded Edition* (Mt. Jackson, VA: Axios Press, 2009).

Running a successful business is always a balancing act. If wages are too low, workers will lose motivation or leave. If wages are too high, profits will be too low to pay for productivity-enhancing investments or other planned expansion. Workers should applaud productivity-enhancing investments, because studies show that, over time, they get all the return on such investments in the form of higher wages, or at least all the return that does not go to customers in the form of lower prices.

It is not surprising, on reflection, that over the years a business's profits and wages tend to rise or fall together, with profits leading a bit, or that this same pattern holds for the economy as a whole. Nor is it surprising that overall employment tends to follow profits, since businesses use profits to invest in workers as well as capital equipment. The only part of profits the workers in general do not directly benefit from is, as noted before, business owners' luxury spending. And of course workers in luxury industries even benefit from that. On balance, a rise in genuine, sustainable profits is very good news for an economy, because it means that higher employment levels and wages will follow sooner or later.

Argument 3 against the Profit System: Quite apart from its injustice and inefficiency, the profit system does not give us the goods that we need. Even when it produces the right goods, it denies them to those who need them the most, the poor.

Private businesses exist to make money. There is a glaring conflict between "production for profit" and "production for people," and under our existing system "production for people" takes the hindmost. As history professor and popular commentator Howard Zinn explained this:

> The profit motive . . . has . . . distorted our whole economic and social system by making profit the key to what is produced and therefore leaving important things unproduced and stupid things produced [as well as] leaving some people rich and some people poor.[42]

Counter-Argument: At first glance, it might seem that the profit system just produces what rich people want, not what the greater number of people need. But this is wrong.

The profit system is guided by profits, and the greatest profits are earned, not by catering to the wants and whims of the rich, but rather by meeting the genuine needs of large numbers of people. Economist Ludwig von Mises explains:

Mass production . . . [is] the fundamental principle of [profit-seeking] industry. . . . Big business, the target of the most fanatic attacks by the so-called leftists, produces . . . for the masses.[43]

Economist Milton Friedman elaborates this point further:

Progress . . . over the past century . . . has freed the masses from backbreaking toil and has made available to them products and services that were formerly the monopoly of the upper classes. . . .[44] The rich in Ancient Greece would have . . . welcomed the improvements in transportation and in medicine, but for the rest, the great achievements of [profit seeking] have redounded primarily to the benefit of the ordinary person.[45]

It is natural to feel that something is very amiss when the profit system stops making shoes before all the poor children have them. But if one looks closely at what is really happening, it will be apparent that profit-making is not to blame.

Nobody wants poor children to go without shoes. But we still operate in an environment of economic scarcity, which means that trade-offs must continually be made. If we keep making shoes, we will have more of them and each pair will be cheaper and cheaper. But then we will have to accept less of something else and higher costs for each unit of that. The only "waste" in the system that one can fairly point to is the portion of rich people's income that is spent on luxuries.

Argument 4 against the Profit System: The uncertain, excessive, and largely undeserved rewards of the profit system encourage business owners to adopt a short-term, thieving mentality.

Counter-Argument: On the contrary, the profit system teaches patience and long-term thinking.

The profit system is not a treasure hunt nor does it encourage short-termism. Most new businesses lose money for a time; entrepreneurs must have faith, patience, and the judgment to know when they are failing and when they are simply suffering the usual setbacks in starting something new.

If profit-seekers have patience, and also the gift of good judgment, they will eventually earn profits, and the profits will start to compound. At first this is a glacially slow process. If $10,000 in starting capital, or in initial profits, grows each year by 12%, it will take twenty years to pass $100,000. But, if the growth rate is maintained, the law of large numbers takes over, and in twenty more years the number will reach $1,000,000. If profits double at a higher rate, such as every six years, they will become a fantastic figure. Such a system can hardly be said to encourage short-termism.

What the profit system does encourage, apart from patience, is to keep growing, keep compounding, no matter how low the rate of annual increase. Britain became the leading economic power, the wonder and envy of the world, from an estimated compound economic growth rate of barely 2% a year from 1780 to 1914.[46] Two percent may not sound impressive to us, but it was far higher than any nation had ever achieved, especially over long periods.

Argument 5 against the Profit System: Profit-driven change is irrational and disorderly.

No one knows where this kind of change will take us, because it is rudderless and unguided. It may not produce progress but instead plunge us into chaos.

Counter-Argument: The profit system is not irrational, disorderly, or chaotic.

A price-and-profit system gives us order, not chaos, an order led and guided by the wishes of consumers. This is a spontaneous order,[47] like the common laws that have accumulated from court cases over the centuries, or rules of grammar or speech.

To think that order cannot exist without a leader's visible commands is natural, but untrue. As economist Friedrich Hayek has written:

> This is not a dispute about whether planning is to be done or not. It is a dispute as to whether planning is

to be done centrally, by one authority for the whole economic system, or is to be divided among many individuals.[48]

We can certainly install a more visible central command, restrict the carrots that seem too sweet, soften the sticks, slow or better regulate the rate of change, but we will get more chaos, not less, and more economic corruption and poverty to boot.

Argument 6 against the Profit System: Economic growth requires cooperation. The profit system discourages cooperation.

Counter-Argument: This is also untrue. The profit system is a form of voluntary cooperation.

It is the most enduring and successful form of human cooperation ever developed. People are naturally both selfish and altruistic, depending on mood and circumstance. They are especially afraid of failure. The profit system incorporates everything genuinely human into the system and produces the most reliable results.

Conclusion: The kind of macroeconomics commonly taught in schools is completely misleading because it ignores the role of profits.

Economist David Ricardo said in the early nineteenth century that "Nothing contributes so much to the prosperity and happiness of a country as high profits."[49]

Ricardo was right, and given the truth of what he said, one must wonder why modern macroeconomists have so little to say about profits. Macroeconomics texts are full of discussion about production growth, employment, inflation, etc., but profits are hardly mentioned. If they are discussed at all, it is generally in the micro-economics section of a text, the part that concerns individual businesses and industries, not the economy as a whole. Economics presented in this way is a falsehood.

13

More on Greed*

I S OUR ENTIRE economy grounded in greed?

Bernie seems to think so. In every speech he rises like a Biblical prophet condemning the greed of corporations and Wall Street, although he arguably undermines his own moral authority by conspicuously omitting any reference to the greed of unions, trial lawyers, or public officials.

Is Bernie right, at least about the market economy? There are many different ways of looking at this issue. We will briefly summarize a few:

---

* The following is a revised and condensed version of text from chapters 13, 14, and 15 from the author's book *Are The Rich Necessary? Great Economic Arguments and How They Reflect Our Personal Values, Updated & Expanded Edition* (Mt. Jackson, VA: Axios Press, 2009).

Argument 1: Both our current political and economic systems are grounded in selfishness and greed and are thus inherently immoral.

Bill Moyers, former assistant to President Lyndon Johnson, later a public television star, warns us about market idolators who wrap themselves in the (American) flag and rely "on your patriotism to distract you from their plunder. While you're standing at attention with your hand over your heart pledging allegiance to the flag, they're picking your pocket."[50]

Marcia Angell, former editor-in-chief of the prestigious *New England Journal of Medicine*, recalls that before the 1980s

> there was something faintly disreputable about really big fortunes. You could choose to do well or you could choose to do good.... That belief was particularly strong among scientists and other intellectuals.[51]

Argument 2: "Greed is good."

Economist John Maynard Keynes, by no means in the "greed is good" camp, thought that greed was at least useful, if only for the time being:

> Avarice and usury must be our gods for a little longer still. For only they can lead us out of the tunnel of economic necessity into daylight.[52]

The most forceful exponent of "greed is good," philosopher and novelist Ayn Rand, held that greed is only menacing outside market environments:

> When money ceases to be the tool by which men deal with one another, then men become the tools of men. Blood, whips, guns—or dollars. Take your choice.[53]

Channeled appropriately through markets, even the most immoderate greed (according to Rand) is only beneficent:

> America's abundance was not created by public sacrifices to "the common good," but by the productive genius of free men who pursued their own personal interests and the making of their own private fortunes. They did not starve the people to pay for America's industrialization. They gave the people better jobs, higher wages, and cheaper goods.[54]

Argument 3: Whether one disapproves or approves of greed has no bearing on economics. Markets are just technical, morally neutral, mechanisms for human exchange.

Milton Friedman took this position when he said that "[What is often referred to as the market] ethic ... cannot in and of itself be regarded as an ethical principle...."[55]

Argument 4: No, the market is not morally neutral, it does express an ethical principle, and that principle is rational self-interest, which should not be confused with greed.

The most famous defense of rational self-interest was offered by the economist Adam Smith in the eighteenth century:

> It is not from the benevolence of the butcher, the brewer, or the baker, that we expect our dinner, but from their regard to their own interest. We address ourselves, not to their humanity but to their self-love, and never talk to them of our own necessities but of their advantages.[56]

> He generally, indeed, neither intends to promote the public interest, nor knows how much he is promoting it. . . . He intends only his own gain, and he is in this, as in many other cases, led by an invisible hand to promote an end which was no part of his intention.[57]

The all-important distinction in Smith's system is between rational and irrational self-interest. The world has had many economic systems based on irrational self-interest, and these bring only misery. For example, consider economic historian David Landes's description of the Ottoman (Turkish) empire of the fourteenth-early twentieth centuries:

> The Ottomans had . . . taken over a region once
> strong, now enfeebled—looting as they went. Now
> they . . . resorted to habit and tried to pillage the in-
> terior, to squeeze their own subjects. Nothing, not
> even the wealth of high officials, was secure. Noth-
> ing could be more self-destructive.[58]

Rational self-interest teaches cooperation rather than predation. As journalist and philosopher Walter Lippmann wrote:

> Until the division of labor had begun to make men
> dependent upon the free collaboration of other men,
> the worldly policy was to be predatory.[59]

Economist David Levy explains how this works in everyday life:

> Under [the profit system], even an insensitive man
> who would not pause to help a blind person across the
> street develops an interest in other people's wants and
> whims when he contemplates investing in a business.[60]

Argument 5: The private market system has its own morality, which is grounded neither in greed nor in rational self-interest.

A young person may think: how glorious to start my own business and be my own boss. But if he or she per-sists in this illusion, the new business will fail, as most do. In order to start and run a successful business, one must be willing, above all, to subordinate oneself in the service of others. One must serve one's customers and one must also serve and respect and nurture one's employees.

Sometimes "bosses" are so talented or lucky that they can seem to get away with either faking or ignoring these requirements. Predation, exploitation, parasitism, or greed may make this transaction, or even this year's profits, fatter. But a business is defined as the present value of all future profits, and these future profits are more often than not ruined by selfishness, even so-called "rational" selfishness.

"Market" values are not easy. They are extremely demanding, and in many cases take generations to learn. It is no coincidence that it was defenders of free markets who led the battle against world slavery and finally won it, against large odds, in the nineteenth century. As economist George Stigler writes:

> Important as the moral influences of the market place are, they have not been subjected to any real study. The immense proliferation of general education, of scientific progress, and of democracy are all coincidental in time and place with the emergence of the free enterprise system of organizing the market place. I believe this coincidence was not accidental.[61]

Economists are often tone deaf about all this. Listen to Geoffrey Martin Hodgson:

> The firm has to compete not simply for profit but for our confidence and trust. To achieve this, it has to abandon

profit-maximization, or even shareholder satisfac-
tion, as the exclusive objectives of the organization.[62]

This is nonsense. How can profits be earned in the
absence of customer and employee confidence and trust?

Perhaps the ultimate wrong note of this kind was
sounded by economist John Kenneth Galbraith, past
president of the American Economic Association, when
he wrote that

> there is nothing reliable to be learned about making
> money. If there were, study would be intense and ev-
> eryone with a positive IQ would be rich.[63]

What Galbraith, like others, failed to see is that one
does not necessarily need a high IQ to make money,
but rather the right personal values, in particular an
ardor to serve others and a degree of realism about
how to do it (since in markets, as in life generally, good
intentions alone do not suffice).

Conclusion

Who is right here? The reader can judge for himself or
herself, but it is clear enough that Bernie's condemna-
tion of corporate and Wall Street greed, while often
quite accurate, is far from a complete picture of America. The most damaging greed occurs when economic
powers on Wall Street team up with powerful government officials in one or another version of today's
crony capitalism, but Bernie is silent about that.

14

Bernie against Trade Agreements

During my 24 years in Congress, I have been proud to stand side by side with the AFL-CIO fighting . . . against disastrous trade agreements like NAFTA, CAFTA, and Permanent Normal Trade Relations with China that have destroyed millions of decent-paying jobs in America.

AFL-CIO Conference, August 18, 2015

You do not have to have a PhD in economics to understand that our unfettered free trade policies have failed.

United Steelworkers Rally, April 29, 2016

I T DETRACTS SOMEWHAT from the message that Bernie delivers these remarks at union gatherings. Is this really a meeting of the minds or just more stroking of and more pandering to the most powerful special interest in Bernie's camp? Perhaps it is both.

Genuine free trade stands in the same relationship to the massive trade agreements of recent years that capitalism stands to crony capitalism. These are opposing categories. Just as free trade is an aspect of capitalism, trade agreements are generally an aspect of crony capitalism.

Referring to trade agreements as "free trade" agreements, as Bernie does, is mistaken. They are anything but. To call them "unfettered free trade" agreements is simply deceptive. Speaking this way is like calling Wall Street a bastion of capitalism or calling the Federal Reserve a bastion of capitalism. People who say these things are either confused or intentionally trying to sow confusion. Part of the reason voters may have trouble understanding all this is that there are so many highly paid and golden tongued spokespeople for special interests intentionally misleading them.

If asked, Bernie would probably state that supporters of both trade agreements and Wall Street are capitalists. He does not wish to acknowledge the distinction between capitalism and crony capitalism, because the latter requires government participation and he prefers to ignore the role of government in creating and fostering the corruption.

Here is another quote from Bernie suggesting that he really does understand that trade agreements are not about "free trade," but instead about government favors and special deals for industries and companies:

> Our trade policies with Mexico, China and other countries have been . . . written by corporate America.
>
> United Steelworkers Rally, April 29, 2016

This is a telling admission. Does Bernie really think that the "greedy" multi-national companies he continually disparages are fans of free trade? If companies write the trade treaties, and they do, along with unions and other special interests, then how can the resulting "deals" and "favors" represent free trade?

We also need to keep in mind that while trade agreements typically focus on some of the more obvious trade barriers, such as tariffs, they typically fail to address a multitude of non-tariff barriers erected by governments. In addition, they overlook the primary trade manipulation tool of our day, which is currency devaluation. When governments or government controlled central banks manipulate a country's currency down, exports are made artificially cheap and imports artificially expensive. There are tremendous trade wars going on right now, but the main weapons are engineered by monetary economists, who are in turn paid well by both governments and special interests. Bernie is largely silent about this.

Bernie does, however, ask:

> Why are we in a race to the bottom with low wage countries like China, Mexico, and India?
>
> AFL-CIO Conference, August 18, 2015

Like other proponents of greater economic equality, Bernie appears confused, or at least unclear, about the respective claims of very poor people abroad versus relatively poor people at home. He wants multinational companies to pay higher wages to the struggling poor in other countries; he invites these workers to come to the US in unlimited numbers; but he opposes allowing the import of more goods made by the same workers.

Below Bernie argues that the NAFTA trade agreement has hurt Mexicans as well as Americans. Since trade agreements are written by special interests, just as Bernie alleges, it is entirely possible for them to hurt both sets of workers.

Bernie:

> Supporters of NAFTA told us it would increase the standard of living in Mexico and significantly reduce the flow of undocumented immigrants into this country as a result. The opposite was true.

> Since the implementation of NAFTA, the number of Mexicans living below the poverty line has increased by over 14 million people. . . . And in the twenty years since NAFTA growth in per capita GDP has been only half of that experienced by other Latin American nations.

> National Association of Latino Elected and Appointed Officials Conference, June 19, 2015

Ironically, in most of his remarks about trade, Bernie sounds very similar to Donald Trump, and strikingly at odds with President Obama and Hillary Clinton:

> We need to stop China from dumping steel into this country by establishing strong countervailing tariffs.
>
> United Steelworkers Rally, April 29, 2016

Over the past three centuries, most economists have argued against high tariffs. In the first place, the preservation or protection of jobs is a dead-end policy. If everyone had preserved and protected their jobs from the Stone Age on, we would all be hunting and gathering.

The most economically thriving US regions tend to have the greatest annual job loss, but also the greatest job creation, with a net gain in both employment and wages. Job turnover can be hard on employees, especially older ones, but it is essential for job growth, economic growth, and an improving standard of living.

In general, nations become rich by learning to innovate, to specialize, and, in global trade, to pursue their comparative advantage. The phrase "comparative advantage" is often misunderstood. It does not mean that a country should find something that it can produce more cheaply than other countries and specialize in that. If a country can produce something more cheaply than any other country, that is called an "absolute advantage," not a comparative advantage. Even if (hypothetically) one country has an absolute advantage in everything and another country has an absolute advantage in nothing, the two can do better by dividing up the tasks and exchanging their work.

In his book *Basic Economics*, Thomas Sowell provides a good example of this. He asks us to assume, for purpose of illustration, that the United States makes both shirts and shoes more cheaply than Canada. In other words, the US has an absolute advantage in both articles. Specifically, the US makes shirts more than twice as cheaply and shoes 25% more cheaply.

Based on these numbers, one might conclude that the US should continue making shirts and shoes for itself, but this would be incorrect. Since the US is much more cost effective in shirts, relatively speaking, than it is in shoes, it will still pay to concentrate on shirts and leave the shoes to Canada. If the US and Canada team up in this way, the total production of shirts and shoes mathematically increases by about 20% and 11% respectively. Just by specializing and trading, the two countries in this hypothetical example become measurably richer.[64]

In this example, US shoe makers will lose jobs and their hardship will be more visible to voters than new shirt making jobs. So far, Sowell has focused on manufacturing. But the same principles apply to the "outsourcing" of service jobs over the internet or telephone lines. The savings achieved by importing electronic services have enabled many companies to prosper, where they otherwise might have stagnated or failed, and thus to hire more employees rather than fewer.[65]

Sowell's exposition of the potential benefits of free trade is logically irrefutable. It must also be noted that there are other benefits of free trade beside comparative advantage. Global companies with a larger market share may be able to achieve economies of scale and thus achieve lower consumer prices than would ever be possible in an autarchic, protectionist world.

Any country that lets other countries enjoy these benefits of scale while it does not is undoubtedly taking a risk. For example, is it wise for the United States, with only four percent of the world's people, to turn over to competitors the other seven billion people in the world as an exclusive market, shut off from us by our own actions?

These are all important questions. But, unfortunately, in the real world, we do not just have a choice between free trade and protectionism. The dominant reality is managed trade, which is more aptly termed crony trade, which generally flies under the false banner of "free trade" even when it is really trying to create, not comparative advantage, but special interest advantage. We live in a muddled or dishonest world.

Should we be surprised that George W. Bush's last treasury secretary, Hank Paulson, has announced that he will vote for Hillary Clinton in 2016 because he believes in "free trade" and "globalism."[66] In order to understand this, we need only recall that Paulson, former CEO of Goldman Sachs, was one of the architects of the Wall Street bailout of 2008 which not only rescued Wall Street, but also rescued his own firm, along with all the shares he still retained in that firm.

We should also keep in mind that it was Goldman Sachs that reportedly paid Hillary $675,000 for three speeches, the transcripts of which she refuses to release.

When Paulson simultaneously endorses "free trade," "globalism," and Hillary, we need to take all this with a grain of salt. To many outside observers, he is a man so deeply enmeshed in crony capitalism and crony trade that he exemplifies both, as does Hillary.

One of the features of trade agreements most highly prized by crony traders is that they may weaken the control of national governments and especially democratically elected national governments. Supra-national organizations such as The World Trade Organization have been granted the authority to overrule all governments, democratic or not.

Moreover, and most importantly, under the guise of "trade rulings," their commands may intrude into issues only tangentially related to trade. It is possible to argue that almost any issue affects trade in some way, so there is little to prevent "mission creep."

A glaring example of this is the present European Union. It began as a "free trade zone" but "mission creep" led it further and further into total control of

Europe. Moreover, its operations were intentionally designed to circumvent voters. All European legislation originates, not in the so-called European Parliament, largely a front body, but rather in the European Commission, a group of well-paid bureaucrats of doubtful expertise who are accountable only to themselves. Although the European Parliament has some power to veto European Commission legislation, it rarely exercises it. The members of this parliament are mostly passed over politicians who enjoy their perks and do as they are told by the Commission.

Gradually the tentacles of this anti-democratic system have spread over Europe, so that today European court decisions trump national court decisions and European Commission rules trump properly enacted democratic legislation. Voters in Europe rejected a "European Constitution" that promised even tighter controls, but the tighter controls were stealthily implemented by the Commission anyway.

This is one of the reasons that Britain finally voted to make a clean break with the European Community. The press and commentators have often falsely portrayed British voters as abandoning free trade. Polls suggest just the opposite. There is an overwhelming consensus in the UK to maintain free trade with Europe if at all possible. What the voters wanted to escape was political control, and unelected political control at that, hiding behind the mask of "free trade."

Critics see the proposed Trans Pacific Partnership (TPP) negotiated by President Obama (but not yet voted on by the US Senate) as a covert attempt to create a Pacific Union modeled on the European Union. This agreement also sets up supra-national bodies with the authority to overrule US courts and legislatures. Donald Trump is opposed. Hillary helped negotiate it and was a staunch supporter. At one time she described it as "the gold standard in trade agreements to open free, transparent, fair trade."[67] When this proved unpopular with Democratic primary voters, she revised that position and announced she did not support it in its "present form." This language was clearly crafted to enable her to resume support for the treaty later. Bernie, to his credit, has always firmly opposed it. As he said:

> We need a movement which will work with the trade union movement to end our disastrous trade policies, and that includes defeating the disastrous TPP.
>
> New Hampshire Democratic Party Convention,
> September 19, 2015

In thinking about a massive crony trade agreement like TPP, we should also keep in mind that real globalization does not require larger and larger centers of political power around the world, whether these centers are continent wide countries or so-called global institutions. There is no reason to believe that vast nation states or other power centers make our world more peaceful. The reverse may be true.

Many larger nations and global institutions are throwbacks to the empires and imperial institutions of the past, such as the Austro-Hungarian or Ottoman or Russian Empires, all of which tried to substitute massive and oppressive bureaucracies for local and participatory government, all of which eventually failed. A multiplicity of small countries, managed on a more human scale, closer to our actual communities, can still trade globally and maintain a global network, even a genuine free trade network. Some of the most skillful members of the present global market today are small countries such as Switzerland and Singapore.

Democracy is far from perfect, but it does give people the right to throw the rulers out and start afresh. Institutions such as the European Community, the United Nations, the World Trade Organization, and the Trans Pacific Partnership (if it comes into existence) may be staffed by people who started their careers with many ideals and every good intention. But freed from voter control, they gradually become ever more remote, pompous, corrupt in soft and hard ways, and ultimately controlled by special interests.

Economist John Maynard Keynes, founder of today's "progressive" economics, was all over the place on the subject of free trade. He joked that he was "a bad bird [saying] one thing one day and something else the next."[68] Bernie is not like that. He is utterly consistent. But he is not giving us a complete picture.

Part Five

Wall Street and the
Federal Reserve

15

Bernie against Wall Street
(The Crash of 2008)

Financial excesses, indeed widespread financial crim-
inality on Wall Street, played a direct role in caus-
ing the world's worst financial crisis since the Great
Depression.

The Urgency of a Moral Economy: Reflections
on the 25th Anniversary of Centesimus Annus,
April 15, 2016

THIS IS CORRECT insofar as it goes, but leaves
out an important part of the story, the role of government in creating and deepening the mess.
The Federal Reserve, Congress, and the president all
contributed to the mess, although the Fed played the
leading role.

On Capitol Hill, Democrats such as Congressman
Barney Frank and Senator Chris Dodd were especially responsible for helping to blow up the housing

bubble preceding the Crash by blocking any attempt to rein in out-of-control government backed mortgage companies such as Fannie Mae and Freddie Mac. Chris Dodd apparently received special favors from a mortgage company. As Michael Burry, hero of the popular film *The Big Short*, noted, the Dodd-Frank Wall Street "reform" legislation that followed was named "for two guys who were bought and paid for by special interests."[69]

President Bush appointed Ben Bernanke as Fed Chairman, and Bernanke in particular fueled the housing bubble by creating far too much new money and keeping interest rates artificially low. The link between too much money and related credit expansion by monetary authorities and bubbles and crashes is not exactly a new or debatable idea. It was first noted by economist John Stuart Mill in 1830 and subsequently elaborated in detail by economist Ludwig von Mises. Here is what Mill said almost two centuries ago:

> An increase of production ... takes place during the progress of [money and credit expansion], as long as the existence of [money and credit expansion] is not suspected. . . . But when the delusion vanishes and the truth is disclosed, those whose commodities are relatively in excess must diminish their production or be ruined: and if during the high prices they have built mills and erected machinery, they will be likely to repent at leisure.[70]

Why does Bernie deliberately omit the role of government in creating first bubble and then bust? As President Bush said, "Wall Street got drunk," but it was Washington that provided the free drinks.

Bernie again:

> Working people lost their jobs, their homes and their savings, while the government bailed out the banks.
>
> > The Urgency of a Moral Economy: Reflections on the 25th Anniversary of Centesimus Annus,
> > April 15, 2016

This part of Bernie's account is all true. The bank bailout was massive. The direct bailout (Troubled Asset Relief Program or TARP) voted by Congress was just the tip of the iceberg. What the Federal Reserve did on its own was far bigger. Investment banks such as Goldman Sachs, speculators par excellence, were re-categorized as deposit-taking banks. This defied common sense, but made them eligible to receive directly the Fed's giveaway money. David Stockman, Budget Director under President Reagan referred to this decision as

a Robin Hood redistribution in reverse.[71]

After that, Ben Bernanke began lending huge sums to Wall Street. Later he claimed that the Fed had lent $1.2 trillion, representing about 9% of the economy's total annual output at the time and 38% of federal government spending. Many experts think this figure is understated. And there were also asset purchases and loan guarantees.*

A study by economists at the University of Missouri-Kansas City funded by the Ford Foundation puts the total of all Fed commitments during the crisis at $29 trillion.[72] This $29 trillion was in addition to commitments by the rest of the government which came to as much as $17 trillion, although a smaller figure was actually spent.[73] Nor did the engineering stop there. After the Fed's balance sheet was increased $1.7 trillion during the crisis, it was increased another $600 billion through what came to be called "quantitative easing," a clunky euphemism for the government printing new money, and another $700 billion by the end of 2012 with no end of the monetary expansion in view.

It is easy to miss the fine print in all of this, which often involves many billions. For example, when the Fed creates new money out of thin air by "buying" government bonds, it then books interest on those bonds. Some of this interest is used to pay Fed expenses, which are neither paid nor approved by Congress, and the rest is sent to the Treasury Department.

In 2012, the "dividend" provided the Treasury in this way amounted to $89 billion.[74] So in effect the government was not only selling bonds to itself. It was also

---

* Some of the facts and text for this chapter are drawn from chapters 11, 15, 18, and 19 of the author's book *Free Prices Now! Fixing the Economy by Abolishing the Fed* (Edinburg, VA: AC2 Books, 2013).

relying on "income" from itself to reduce its reported budget deficit.

Although Bernie directly comments on none of this, and says that he does not approve of the bank bailouts, it appears that he is unaware of the Fed's role in creating the bubble and generally approves of the Fed's role in driving up debt, even though most of the new loans go to Wall Street at giveaway prices.

It is also hard to understand why anyone would think that creating massive amounts of new debt would really help us recover from a Crash. If too much bad debt caused the problem, which leads to a crash, how will piling on even more new debt help to solve it? If large amounts of money have been wasted on unwise borrowing and spending, why will it help to waste even more? Economist Friedrich Hayek has noted that

> to combat the depression by [printing more money and encouraging more debt] is to attempt to cure the evil by the very means which brought it about.[75]

Hayek continues:

> The same stabilizers who believed that nothing was wrong with the boom and that it might last indefinitely because [consumer] prices did not rise, now believe that everything could be set right again if only we would use the [same] weapons of monetary policy.[76]

President Obama in his first budget message said: "We are moving from an era of borrow and spend to one of save and invest." Both his and the Fed's actions certainly belied these words.

Why then did the government bail out the banks? The stated reason was to avoid a depression for the economy. This really meant getting through the next election which was only a few months away. President Bush and many in Congress no doubt accepted this story at face value. But it is very doubtful that bankruptcies on Wall Street would have brought down the Main Street economy, and quite illogical to think that a bailout would solve the problem.

We also must keep in mind that loss and bankruptcy are a natural, inescapable, and ultimately healthy part of the free price and profit system. When companies fail, their assets do not disappear. They are bought at cheap prices by more capable companies and put to better use.

When government interferes with this process, it does not prevent economic failure; it just prolongs and deepens it by preventing the needed cleaning out process. The result is "zombie" companies lingering in a "zombie" economy where the unresolved wreckage of past mistakes prevents complete recovery and a return to full employment, often with new and better paying jobs.

What else contributed to the government's panicked decision to bail out Wall Street? Campaign contributions no doubt played a large role. But there were larger, much larger considerations also at stake.

Both government and Wall Street go to great pains to maintain the fiction that banking is part of a market system. It is not. It is strictly a department of government whose principal role is to sell government debt. Moreover the rules that have been established for it make no sense, so it is forever in crisis. A department of government, it is also a ward of government.

Banks can be counted on to play their assigned role of buying and reselling US government debt in massive quantities. They know that failure to do so will destroy their co-dependent relationship with Washington. Just as they need Washington, so Washington needs them.

Note that it is illegal for the Fed to buy government bonds directly with its newly created money. If it did, the government would be "borrowing" from itself. But after the bonds are sold to Wall Street, the Fed can then buy them back, which amounts to the same thing.

Through this process, the Fed has become the largest creditor to the government, which means in plain language that the government has become the largest creditor to itself, larger even than Japan or China. This can only be described as a massive fraud and shell game, but one that absolutely depends on Wall Street's participation and connivance.

The Wall Street wards are of course well rewarded for their services. They have first access to all the new money being printed by the Fed, and can either speculate with it or lend it on. When securities market prices fall, or threaten to fall, the Fed supports them. The Fed does not of course admit that its market intervention is supporting Wall Street. It pretends that it is doing this to help the rest of us. But there is not a shred of economic evidence or logic to support its actions. It is just crony capitalism carried to an extreme.

A complicating factor in this delicate dance between Wall Street and Washington is that US banks are only required to hold a maximum 10% reserve against customer deposits and often less. One of the first actions of the Federal Reserve when it came into being in 1914 was to lower reserves, and it has been lowering them ever since. This assumes that depositors will never demand more than 10% of their funds back at any one time.

If this calculation proves to be wrong, the bank will be unable to repay depositors as promised. Because of the vanishing deposit requirement, known in the industry as a fractional reserve, banks are technically insolvent all the time. They are an accident waiting to happen.

These problems were further compounded in the years immediately preceding the Crash of 2008 by a new regulatory requirement called, with unintended irony, "mark to market." Regulators intended that bank assets would reflect market prices, which would make it more apparent which banks were financially sound. But since there are no actual market prices in banking, this new rule created chaos. If one type of loan for $1,000 had been sold by a bank for $100, then all such loans were required to be marked down 90%, and on this basis very few banks could claim to be solvent.

When this nonsensical rule came into effect, the Crash of 2008 began; when the rule was tabled, the Crash almost immediately ended. Tabling the rule had a much more dramatic effect on ending the crisis than anything else the government did. Despite the chaos, Fed chairman Bernanke argued to keep the rule, and his opposition to ending it more than any other factor prolonged the stock market rout, even as the Fed was otherwise trying to support the market.

Bernie again:

> We have seen on Wall Street that financial fraud became not only the norm but in many ways the new business model. Top bankers have shown no shame for their bad behavior. . . . The billions and billions of dollars of fines they have paid for financial fraud are just another cost of doing business.
>
> The Urgency of a Moral Economy: Reflections on the 25th Anniversary of Centesimus Annus, April 15, 2016

This is also true, but note that even the fines have been tempered by crony arrangements. After President Obama's election, he met at the White House with top Wall Street officials and allegedly began by saying that his administration was "the only thing between you and the pitchforks." This was interpreted as a brazen demand for campaign contributions and other support, and Wall Street immediately complied. Perhaps as a direct result, the large scale indictments of Wall Street leaders that were expected never materialized.

Bernie again:

> It is not acceptable that hedge fund managers pay a lower effective tax rate than nurses or truck drivers.
>
> On Democratic Socialism in the United States,
> November 19, 2015

This is literally true, but arguably misleading. It does not mean that the rich in general pay a lower tax rate than ordinary workers. It means that a certain class of Wall Street investors enjoy a tax loophole that treats much of their ordinary income as a capital gain, which is taxed at a lower rate. Everyone understands that this is a loophole engineered and protected by powerful Democratic New York legislators such as then senator Hillary Clinton and current Senate Democratic Minority Leader Chuck Schumer. Bernie is right to oppose it.

Bernie:

> The huge financial institutions must be broken up.
>
> National Association of Latino Elected and
> Appointed Officials Conference, June 19, 2015

They would have broken themselves up if not bailed out in 2008. If all federal subsidies and related rules were withdrawn and Wall Street allowed to operate on genuine market lines, this would take care of itself.

Economics is admittedly a confusing subject. A writer for the devotedly "progressive" *New Yorker* magazine proclaimed in September 2009 that Alan Greenspan and Ben Bernanke were Republicans who had followed a

> free-market [policy]

of keeping

> interest rates exceptionally low.[77]

This is absurd. A government price manipulation cannot be called a free market policy. Nor is Ben Bernanke even a Republican. After leaving the Fed, where he had been appointed by President George W. Bush, he changed his party affiliation to Democrat, and began earning large "speaking fees" (Hillary and Bill Clinton style) from the banks and companies he had bailed out.

16

Bernie Falls Down on Fed

THERE WAS ALMOST no discussion of the actions or role of the Federal Reserve during the presidential primary campaigns of 2016, including Bernie's campaign, although Bernie said more about it than just about any other candidate, with the possible exception of Senator Rand Paul. This is curious, since the Fed has played such a central and activist role in managing the economy for the last few decades and especially since the Crash of 2008, the subject of the last chapter.

Bernie voted for Congressman Ron Paul's Audit the Fed bill, which would have at least reduced a bit the shroud of secrecy surrounding the Fed, but he clearly does not agree with Paul's proposal to abolish the agency, nor does he seem to agree with Paul that the

Fed has created too much money and credit and in the process condemned the US economy, and especially its vulnerable poor or middle class citizens, to an endless cycle of ever widening bubbles and busts. When the Fed began talking about finally increasing interest rates, after keeping them near zero since 2008, Bernie opposed this step, even though the new Fed money is provided to Wall Street first at giveaway rates .

Bernie's most explicit account of his view of the Fed is contained in a *New York Times* Op Ed piece published in December 2015, just after the Fed raised the Fed Funds rate by a quarter point. The Op Ed blasted this decision, said that rates should not be raised until unemployment fell to 4%, and added that:

> The recent decision by the Fed to raise interest rates is the latest example of the rigged economic system. Big bankers and their supporters in Congress have been telling us for years that runaway inflation is just around the corner. They have been dead wrong each time. Raising interest rates now is a disaster for small business owners who need loans to hire more workers and Americans who need more jobs and higher wages. . . . Raising interest rates should only be done as a last resort, not to fight phantom inflation.

As we shall discuss, this idea that easy Fed money helps workers defies the facts.

Bernie went on to characterize the Fed as a stooge of Wall Street:

> The sad reality is that the Federal Reserve doesn't regulate Wall Street; Wall Street regulates the Fed.

Bernie makes a good point here. The Fed and Wall Street are like Siamese twins. Washington, the Fed, and Wall Street are all conjoined. But government, in particular the Fed, is the senior partner, and in no sense the stooge, as we shall also discuss.

Bernie continued:

> It's time to make banking work for the productive economy and for all Americans, not just a handful of wealthy speculators. And it begins by making the Federal Reserve a more democratic institution, one that is responsive to the needs of ordinary Americans rather than the billionaires on Wall Street. . . . Banking industry executives must no longer be allowed to serve on the Fed's boards and to hand-pick its members and staff. Board positions should instead include representatives from all walks of life—including labor, consumers, homeowners, urban residents, farmers and small businesses.

Bernie has a point here too. Bankers should not have automatic rights to board seats. But it is not bankers who control the main Fed board these days; it is PhD economists appointed by the President. As a result, economic writer James Grant jokes that we have replaced the "gold standard" with a "PhD standard." Based on what the Fed has done in recent years, almost anybody from Bernie's list would be an improvement, although choosing people as representatives of special interests such as "labor" or "small business" would just exacerbate the crony capitalist mess the Fed has become.

Bernie again:

> Government should "create good jobs" by stopping commercial banks from "gambling with the bank deposits of the American people," by ordering the Fed to "stop providing incentives for banks to keep money out of the economy," and by "demanding that large banks agree to more . . . lending to creditworthy small businesses and consumers, reducing credit card interest rates and fees, and providing help to underwater and struggling homeowners."

Bernie added that the Glass-Steagall Act, which, until repeal by the Clinton administration, separated deposit taking banks from Wall Street investment firms, should be re-enacted and that "full and unredacted" minutes of Fed meetings should be released within six months rather than five years.[78]

Re-enactment of Glass-Steagall would be an improvement, and so would more transparency in Fed minutes. But Bernie's overall position is contradictory, in that the "easy money" policy he prefers cannot help the poor and middle class as the system is currently operated.

As we noted in the last chapter, when the Fed creates masses of new money, it initially flows to Wall Street, which profits from it in a variety of ways, but from there its path is unpredictable. One of the simplest ways that

Wall Street profits from this new money is to deposit it back with the Fed in return for modest interest. The Fed made this possible by inserting into the TARP bill in 2008 a novel authority for the Agency to pay interest on bank reserves. Of course this interest is paid by creating even more new money, but it provides an incentive for banks to leave reserves idle. In this case, the money does not actually go anywhere.

On the other hand, the reserves are not as idle as they look. For example, they support derivatives activity (securities that trade on other securities). The total amount of derivatives held by the top four US banks is estimated at the moment to be over $200 trillion. And keep in mind that it was derivatives exposure that brought the investment firm Lehman Brothers down in 2008, at the beginning of the Crash.

In addition to promoting the TARP bill in Congress in 2008, the Fed also resorted to numerous other ways of flooding the economy with money and credit, some of which were clearly illegal, because they exceeded the authority granted under the Federal Reserve Act. The purchase of Fannie Mae and Freddie Mac securities in particular was unauthorized and therefore illegal.

To the degree that the new money created by the Fed eventually gets beyond Wall Street, that is, gets out into the general economy, it flows in different directions and has different effects. If it reaches the average consumer, it may produce consumer price inflation. This does seem to be happening to a degree. Consumer price inflation calculated as it has been in the past (before changes by the Clinton administration) would be much higher than the level currently reported by the Commerce Department.

If the new money reaches rich people, it drives up the prices of what rich people buy. We see this today when a single townhouse in Manhattan is listed for sale at over $100 million. If it flows into the stock market, it raises stock prices. If enough flows in this direction, it creates an asset bubble, which appears to be happening once again today. Asset bubbles are followed by crashes, which in turn bring recession and unemployment. Recession and unemployment hit the poor and middle class hardest. Bernie does not seem to understand any of this.

Wherever the new money flows, it may increase demand in the short run, only to reduce it in the long run. This is because the Fed does not just give the new money away. It takes the form of debt. A little debt, especially if invested wisely, may help an economy. But too much or poorly invested debt strangles it. Some Fed economists respond to this by suggesting that the Fed should start giving money away. But how can money maintain any value if given away?

As consumers, businesses, and governments become weighed down with more and more debt from the past, especially debt dollars that were wasted, the interest and principal payments become increasingly burdensome. Dollars that might have been spent on new investments with the potential to create new jobs and new income are instead siphoned off to pay for past mistakes.

Historically we can measure how many dollars of economic growth we get from each new dollar of debt in the economy. At the moment, the math on this is negative. In other words, more new debt leads to less, not more, economic growth and jobs.

Despite this plain evidence, the Fed continues to try to persuade consumers and businesses to increase their borrowing and spending and also underwrites government borrowing and spending. It holds interest rates very low, which for the moment keeps the debt house of cards from tumbling down.

Economist Adam Smith anticipated the chaos created by the Fed almost 250 years ago when he wrote:

> The statesman who should attempt to direct private people in what manner they ought to employ their capitals, would . . . assume an authority . . . which would nowhere be so dangerous as in the hands of a man who had folly and presumption enough to fancy himself fit to exercise it.[79]

Smith is right: no person or institution can succeed as a central economic planner. The fall of the Soviet Union should have driven home this message, but since then the central planners at the Fed have been given ever more power. The US operated quite successfully without a central bank for almost a century. This was the golden age of American economic growth and also a period of overall price stability, despite many ups and downs along the way.

Paul Volcker, arguably the most successful Fed chairman, said that

> if the overriding objective is price stability, we did a better job with the nineteenth century gold standard and passive central banks, with currency boards or even "free banking."[80]

In making this statement, he may have been referring to the 97% loss of dollar purchasing power since the Fed began operations in 1914.

Moreover, the stench of economic corruption surrounding any central bank is becoming more and more noticeable at the Fed, as evidenced by the bank bailouts but much else besides. President Andrew Jackson warned about this in his 1832 message vetoing the rechartering of the Second Bank of the United States, the US central bank of his day:

> It is to be regretted that the rich and powerful too often bend the acts of government to their selfish purposes. Distinctions in society will always exist under every just government. Equality of talents, of education, or of wealth cannot be produced by human institutions. In the full enjoyment of the

gifts of Heaven and the fruits of superior industry,
economy, and virtue, every man is equally entitled
to protection by law; but when the laws undertake
to add to these natural and just advantages artifi-
cial distinctions, to grant titles, gratuities, and exclusive privileges, to make the rich richer and the
potent more powerful, the humble members of society—the farmers, mechanics, and laborers—who
have neither the time nor the means of securing like
favors to themselves, have a right to complain of the
injustice of their Government.

Many of our rich men have not been content with
equal protection and equal benefits, but have be-
sought us to make them richer by act of Congress....
It is time to pause in our career to review our principles.... If we cannot at once, in justice to interests vested under improvident legislation, make our
Government what it ought to be, we can at least
take a stand against all new grants of monopolies
and exclusive privileges, against any prostitution of
our Government to the advancement of the few at
the expense of the many.[81]

Jackson does not mention in his formal message
that he was also suspicious of the role of central banks
in blowing up economic bubbles. He had apparently
intuited this central truth of monetary economics by
reading about the South Sea Bubble in France (1711–
1720). Unfortunately, he failed to see that central banks
and related attempts of government to manipulate the

currency are not the sole cause of bubbles, that fractional reserve banking practices were also at fault. But he was right that eliminating central banks would make bubbles more self-limiting and thus less potentially catastrophic.

As in so many areas, Bernie clearly sees that something is very wrong with the Fed. But he does not give us the whole story.

Part Six

Lessons from the Past

17

Bernie for Franklin Roosevelt (The Great Depression)

W HEN BERNIE LOOKS back through American history, he sees many parallels between 1928, the eve of the Great Depression, and today, especially in the growing inequality that characterized both eras:

> Today, we live in the wealthiest nation in the history of the world, but that reality means little because almost all of that wealth is controlled by a tiny handful of individuals. America now has more income and wealth inequality than any major country on earth, and the gap between the very rich and everyone else is wider than at any time since the 1920s.
>
> National Urban League, July 31, 2015

Bernie draws his conclusion about rapidly rising inequality, in the 1920s and today, from a website that in turn appears to draw its data from a 2014 book, *Capital in the 21st Century*, by the young French economist Thomas Piketty. A reviewer of that book described Piketty as the man "who exposed capitalism's fatal flaw." The Obama White House, the Council on Foreign Relations, and the International Monetary Fund all rolled out the red carpet for the author when he visited the US for a book tour sponsored by his publisher, Harvard University Press.

So what is this flaw? Supposedly under capitalism the rich get steadily richer in relation to everyone else; inequality gets worse and worse. It is all baked into the cake, utterly unavoidable.

To support this thesis, Piketty offers some contorted and unsupported financial logic, but also what he calls "a spectacular graph" of historical data. What does the graph actually show?

The amount of US income controlled by the top 10% of earners starts at about 40% in 1910, rises to about 50% before the Crash of 1929, falls thereafter, returns to about 40% in 1995, and thereafter rises again to about 50% before falling somewhat after the Crash of 2008. Data from after the book's publication indicates that the 50% level was again reached by 2012.

Let's think about what this really means. Relative income of the top 10% did not rise inexorably over this period. Instead it peaked at two times: just before the great crashes of 1929 and 2008 and to a slightly less degree before the Dot-com Crash of 2000. In other words, inequality rose during the great economic bubble eras and fell during the subsequent crashes.

And what caused and characterized these bubble eras? As we have already noted, they were principally caused by the US Federal Reserve creating far too much new money and debt. They were also characterized by an explosion of crony capitalism as some rich people exploited all the new money, both on Wall Street and through connections with the government in Washington.

We can learn a great deal about crony capitalism by studying the period between the end of World War I and the Great Depression and also the last twenty years, but we won't learn much about capitalism. Crony capitalism is the opposite of capitalism. It is a perversion of the market system, not the result of free prices and free markets.

One can see why the White House likes Piketty. He supports their narrative that government is the cure for inequality when in reality government has been the principal cause of growing inequality.

The White House and IMF also love Piketty's proposal, not only for high income taxes, but also for substantial wealth taxes. The IMF in particular has been beating a drum for wealth taxes as a way to restore government finances around the world and also to reduce economic inequality.

Proponents of a massive wealth tax often promise that it would be a "one-time" event that would not be repeated, but that would actually help economic growth by reducing economic inequality.

This is nonsense. Economic growth is produced when a society saves money and invests the savings wisely. It is not quantity of investment that matters most, but quality. Government is capable neither of saving nor investing, much less investing wisely.

Nor should anyone imagine that a wealth tax program would be a "one-time" event. No tax is ever a one-time event. Once established, it would not only persist; it would steadily grow over the years.

Piketty should also ask himself a question that we discussed in an earlier chapter. What will happen when investors have to liquidate their stocks, bonds, real estate, or other assets in order to pay the wealth tax? How will markets absorb all the selling? Who will be the buyers? And how will it help economic growth for markets and asset values to collapse under the selling pressure?

Bernie also has his own interpretation of the Great Depression and the Franklin D. Roosevelt administration. Roosevelt is clearly Bernie's hero and role model:

> In his inaugural remarks in January 1937, in the midst of the Great Depression, President Franklin Delano

> Roosevelt looked out at the nation and . . . saw one-third of a nation ill-housed, ill-clad, ill-nourished. . . .
>
> And [Roosevelt] acted. Against the ferocious opposition of the ruling class of his day, people he called economic royalists, [the president] implemented a series of programs that put millions of people back to work, took them out of poverty and restored their faith in government. He redefined the relationship of the federal government to the people of our country. He combatted cynicism, fear and despair. He reinvigorated democracy. He transformed the country.
>
> And that is what we have to do today.
>
> On Democratic Socialism in the United States,
> November 19, 2015

There are many questions to be asked about this version of the Great Depression. The Roosevelt speech Bernie quotes is not from the first inaugural, but from the second. Why was unemployment and misery still at depression levels four years after Bernie's hero took office? And why did the economy take a further nose dive only a year after that speech?

Why did Treasury Secretary Henry Morgenthau, President Franklin Roosevelt's close friend and heartfelt progressive, admit before Congress in 1939 that government leadership of the economy had not rescued us from the Great Depression:

> I want to see this country prosperous. I want to see people get enough to eat. We have never made good

> on our promises.... I say after eight years of this ad-
> ministration we have just as much unemployment as
> when we started and an enormous debt to boot.[82]

Here is a quite different version of the Great Depression from an earlier book by this author. It does not
rate Roosevelt as a hero and savior, but as someone who
made a miserable situation far, far worse:*

When the inflationary bubble fueled by the Fed during World War I burst in the Depression of 1920–1921,
the Fed had not yet fully developed its current methods, and chose not to intervene to prop up prices. Both
prices and the economy plunged precipitously, but then
righted themselves and recovered. The Depression
was over in only a year and a half, in sharp contrast to
what happened after the Crash of 1929. In 1920–1921,
the Fed actually raised interest rates while the Harding
administration cut government spending dramatically
in order to balance the budget. All of this is directly
contrary to current Fed (Keynesian) doctrine, but the
record speaks for itself. By 1923, unemployment in the
US was only 2.4%.[83] An excellent book on this subject
is *The Forgotten Depression* by James Grant.

During the 1920s, Benjamin Strong, head of the
New York Fed, developed some of the present credit

---

* Some of the facts and text for this chapter are drawn from chapters 15
and 30 of the author's book *Free Prices Now! Fixing the Economy by
Abolishing the Fed* (Edinburg, VA: AC2 Books, 2013).

expansion techniques ("open market policy"), in order to "stimulate" and "manage" the economy. In 1927, the boom (actually bubble) seemed to be faltering, so Strong decided to

give a little coup de whiskey to the stock market.[84]

This miscalculation, not unlike Ben Bernanke's lowering of interest rates in 2007, contributed to the Crash that followed.

After the Crash of 1929, first President Hoover and then President Roosevelt acted vigorously to prevent employers from reducing wages. Wages are of course among the most important prices of the economy. Since the final price of goods was plunging, an inability to reduce wages meant that many companies faced almost certain bankruptcy. The only way to prevent this was to lay off employees on a massive scale.

Ironically, those employees not laid off got the equivalent of enormous raises. The reason was that pre-crash wages, in effect frozen by the government, could buy much more because of the then reduced prices of all consumer goods. In this way, some workers, especially unionized workers supported by the Roosevelt administration, got a windfall while millions of others became homeless or went hungry.

Roosevelt undertook other measures that deepened the Depression as well. He put the National Recovery Administration (NRA) in charge of industry. The

NRA tried to control all prices and wages with an iron hand. In a famous incident, a New Jersey immigrant worker, Jacob Maged, was sentenced to jail for three months on a charge of pressing a suit for 35 cents instead of the legislatively required 40 cents.

The NRA also demanded that labor unions be given a role in company management. Until the NRA was ruled unconstitutional by the Supreme Court, many businesses expected to be nationalized. The administration increased taxes and even announced that it would pass legislation to tax profits, until the 1937 Crash persuaded Roosevelt that he had better leave alone the meager profits surviving companies could eke out.

Following World War II, many people, including many economists, expected the economy to fall back into depression. They argued against ending wartime price and wage controls and also against reducing government expenditure and taxes. Fortunately this advice was not followed. General price and wage controls were abandoned, government spending was cut 70% by 1948, joint income tax filing was introduced, which at that time reduced income taxes, and many business and excise taxes were eliminated.

As a result, the return of 10 million veterans did not drive up unemployment. This remained below 5% until the recession of 1949 temporarily raised it to 6%. These figures were far, far better than anything achieved by the Keynesian policies employed before the war during the Great Depression.[85]

The monumental crash of Japan in the late 1980s following an earlier bubble is particularly instructive, because that crash presaged later crashes in the US and Europe, and because the Japanese government followed standard Keynesian doctrine in its response. Several decades later, the Japanese economy is still depressed, and so much new government debt has been created that tax receipts barely cover debt service (even at artificially repressed interest rates) and social security payments.

In sharp contrast, other Asian economies that crashed in the late 1990s side-stepped the standard Keynesian "remedies" and recovered swiftly. Their example should have been studied more closely. Following the Crash of 2008, most countries ignored it and sought to apply the standard Keynesian remedies of printing money and piling new bad debt on old. Only a few, such as Latvia and Estonia, did not, and they have relatively low unemployment today.[86]

Has President Obama or Bernie or Hillary Clinton learned anything from this? Apparently not. In 2014's state of the union address, Obama took a leaf out of Hoover's and Roosevelt's book by calling for higher minimum state and federal wages and higher wages in general: "I ask ... America's business leaders to ... raise [all] your employees' wages."

Hillary Clinton echoed this in a June 2016 campaign speech when she said:

> My mission as President will be to help create more good-paying jobs so we can get incomes rising for hard-working families across America.... It's a pretty simple formula: higher wages lead to more demand, which leads to more jobs with higher wages. And I've laid out a detailed agenda to jumpstart this virtuous cycle.

Unfortunately, Hillary's formula is economic nonsense, as many economists have explained since the tragic misuse of these ideas by both Hoover and Roosevelt during the Depression. If Hillary thinks that raising wages will help, why not just legislate that all wages in the US must be tripled by employers. See how well that goes. It cannot work because the market left alone adjusts wages and other costs to prices to maximize employment. Any intervention by ignorant politicians will just destroy the balance of costs and prices and thus cause devastating unemployment.

As noted above, the Hoover/Roosevelt embrace of these quack economic remedies meant that some workers, especially union members, got a windfall while others got destitution. The same thing happened when the Obama administration bailed out General Motors. It was not only the shareholders and bond holders who lost out when the administration gave the union ownership of the company. The non-unionized workers, even those in the most efficient plants, lost everything: jobs and retirement benefits. Unionized workers allied with the president kept what they had and the union got the windfall of company ownership to boot.

In the same 2014 State of the Union speech, the president did not just ask employers to raise wages. He also required them to pay a higher minimum wage if they had a federal contract. Hearing this, employers could only wonder what further wage controls he would propose next if they did not keep up their campaign contributions.

If more federal wage controls do come, it is not even clear that layoffs could be used as in the 1930s to save businesses from bankruptcy. Economist Paul Krugman has proposed federal controls on the right to lay off or fire workers. President Obama has also proposed giving workers the right to sue if they apply for a job and are turned down.

The state of the economy provides sufficient reason for business managers to be cautious about hiring. The Federal Reserve's low interest rate policy and regulatory rules make it very difficult to persuade a bank to finance expansion. And Obamacare creates a strong disincentive to hire the fiftieth employee.

With this kind of political background, why would any employer risk hiring a new worker if not absolutely necessary? This is especially true for small businesses, and small businesses have always been the chief source of new jobs.

There is a larger lesson here. To thrive, an economy needs free prices. Free prices not only provide the truthful signals that producers and consumers need in order to make good decisions. They also provide the discipline that any economic system requires.

Fixing the economy is not all that difficult. All we have to do is let producers and consumers sort out prices together and the engine of job growth will start up. Meanwhile President Obama's, Hillary's, and Bernie's fond embrace of the failed policies of Franklin Roosevelt just make it harder.

Bernie does not discuss any of this, because it does not fit his world view. He believes what he was told as a child, that Hoover created the Great Depression and Roosevelt fixed it, despite the irrefutable evidence that the Great Depression lasted for over a decade, unlike the 1920 Depression which, left alone, was over in a year and a half.

18

Bernie for LBJ's Great Society

In the 1960s, President Johnson passed Medicare and Medicaid to provide healthcare to millions of senior citizens and families with children, persons with disabilities and some of the most vulnerable people in this county. Once again these vitally important programs were derided by the right wing as socialist programs that were a threat to our American way of life.

On Democratic Socialism in the United States,
November 19, 2015

BERNIE DOES NOT say too much about the specific programs that in some cases were started by President Roosevelt and in other cases were started or expanded by President Johnson. He just takes for granted that they have been hugely successful and should be further expanded. He does occasionally single out Medicare and Medicaid and Social Security as some of the best legislation ever passed, but it is clear he endorses the entire Great Society program and wishes to build on it.

At this point, almost a century has elapsed since Roosevelt and a half century since Johnson signed all his legislation including the famous "War on Poverty." There is plenty of evidence with which to reach a judgment about whether the social welfare policies so ardently embraced by Bernie have actually worked.

Mitt Romney said during the 2012 presidential campaign: "I'm not concerned about the very poor. We have a safety net there. If it needs repair, I'll fix it." But can there really be any doubt that it needs fixing?

Unfortunately the government does not provide any reliable numbers to help us with this question. The biggest federal poverty program, the Earned Income Tax Credit (EITC) pays 27 million taxpayers $60 billion in cash. The government admits it is riddled with fraud. Like Section 8 housing vouchers and Medicaid, EITC payments are also excluded when the government totes up who is poor and who is not.

It is obvious that the ranks of the poor swelled during and after the Crash of 2008. Average income fell during the Crash and has since fallen more. Economist Paul Krugman is right to call it a "rich man's recovery." If unemployment figures were calculated in the same way as in the 1930s, public officials could no longer deny that 2008 brought a depression, not a recession.

The government is also unclear, it would seem intentionally so, about how much it spends in total on the poor. A Senate subcommittee struggled to estimate total spending on the poor and came up with a number of $61,194 per impoverished household per year.

This number is misleading because it includes people who are only temporarily poor, such as students using federal Pell grants for their education, but is still almost three times the federally defined poverty threshold for a family of four. If we take medical spending out, it is still twice the poverty threshold.

Since all this money is clearly not going to the poor, where is it going? A lot of it is presumably supporting well paid federal workers, or indirectly state and local workers, all of whom are in turn protected by powerful public unions.

If we take all federal transfer payments, not just those specifically earmarked for poverty programs, only 36% of the money is reaching the bottom 20% of households by income and even less is reaching the truly poor. And even these figures do not count all the federal subsidies for corporations or the rich.

Almost all the numbers we get from the federal government are either poorly designed, or are well designed to confuse and hide the truth about what is going on. Looking behind the smokescreens, one thing is obvious about all federal poverty programs. They not only create disincentives to work. They actually tax work at horrific rates.

As economist Thomas Sowell has explained:

> Someone who is trying to climb out of poverty by working their way up can easily reach a point where a $10,000 increase [in pay] can cost them $15,000 in lost benefits they no longer qualify for. That amounts to a marginal tax rate of 150 percent—far more than millionaires pay.[87]

This outrageous tax on the poor has been made even worse by Obamacare. A worker can earn just a few dollars more, and find that more than $10,000 in medical insurance subsidy has vanished. Obamacare also in effect adds $2.28–$5.89 to the cost of hiring a minimum wage worker, thereby creating another major barrier to work, a subject we will explore further in a subsequent chapter.

Has the war on poverty been a success? No. Does the safety net for the poor desperately need fixing? Yes.

Leading policy analyst John Goodman of Southern Methodist University has estimated that "if there had never been a welfare state [in the US], economic growth alone should have virtually eliminated poverty by now." Goodman also adds an interesting note about how progressives who designed and expanded this welfare state have become increasingly reactionary in the face of failure:

> If you are one of the folks who voted [as a progres-
> sive] in the [2012] election, what did you vote for? . . .
> Here are three things for starters: (1) no reform of the
> public schools, (2) no reform of the welfare systems,
> and (3) no reform of labor market institutions that
> erect barriers between new entrants and good jobs.

All these policies are on top of Federal Reserve and government regulatory actions that keep driving up consumer prices. By definition, the poor, who have the least money, suffer the most from these rising prices.

If voters really want to help the poor, they will have to start by admitting that we need some new ideas. Bernie says the same thing: that we need new ideas. But his ideas are as old as Presidents Roosevelt's and Johnson's and seem not to have changed over the course of his long life.

Part Seven

Fixing What's Broken

19

Bernie for Jobs for All

It makes far more sense to put millions of people back to work rebuilding our crumbling infrastructure, than to have a real unemployment rate of almost 10%.

> On Democratic Socialism in the United States,
> November 19, 2015

We need to create at least 13 million new jobs over the next five years rebuilding our crumbling roads, bridges, water systems, wastewater plants, dams, culverts, railways, airports, broadband and electric grid. And we will make sure that all of the steel that goes into this $1 trillion [over five years] jobs plan is made in America, not in China.

> United Steelworkers Rally, April 29, 2016

One in four construction workers are Latino, and the fastest way to increase jobs is to rebuild our crumbling infrastructure. . . .

We also need to address the crisis of youth unemployment. The real unemployment rate for young Hispanic college graduates is 11%, nearly double the rate of white Americans. For young Hispanics with only a high school degree, the real unemployment rate is 36%.

More than 50,000 Latinos turn 18 every month, and the time is long overdue for us to start investing in our young people, to help them get the jobs and training they need, the education they deserve, so that they can be part of the middle class. . . . I recently introduced legislation to provide $5.5 billion in immediate funding to States and localities to employ 1 million young Americans between the ages of 16 and 24, and provide job training to hundreds of thousands of other young Americans.

National Association of Latino Elected and
Appointed Officials Conference, June 19, 2015

BERNIE TELLS EVERYONE, especially labor union audiences and minority groups, that government spending will restore the middle class and end unemployment. Can it? Is there any evidence this will succeed? How does Bernie know that a $1 trillion public works expenditure will create 13,000 new jobs? How does he know that each new job will cost $76,000? And is it fair that only union members will be eligible for these jobs, because of current rules instituted by President Obama?

One way to explore these questions is to look at the record of President Obama's Stimulus Act, passed early in his first term as president. He promised at that time that the stimulus would focus on infrastructure investments. But stimulus spending is an act of government, and therefore becomes immediately politicized. Every special interest stakes some claim, so that the actual direction the money takes is impossible to predict. In the end, most of the spending was not on infrastructure.

President Obama also promised that his bill would be free of Congressional earmarks ("pork" for individual members of Congress) and later, after the bill passed, boasted that he had kept it clean. He had not.

Speaker of the House Nancy Pelosi got a special wetlands provision for her district. Senate Majority Leader Harry Reid (D-Nevada) got billions for a high-speed rail connection from Los Angeles to Las Vegas. The House bill had nothing at all for high-speed transit. The Senate bill had $2 billion. The Congressional committee that was charged with reconciling $0 and $2 billion "compromised" at $8 billion.[88] This must have been a Congressional first and reflected Senator Reid's power.

In addition to the stealth earmarks, the bill had lots of non-germane spending such as $246 million in targeted tax breaks for Hollywood and $198 million for aging Filipino World War II veterans, many not living in the US.[89] One of the non-germane provisions required that all medical records be computerized and made available to the government and other private parties with no opt-out for privacy. The data would be used by the government to evaluate both the effectiveness and cost-effectiveness of medical procedures, which would facilitate government control over medicine.

This provision, like others, had nothing to do with economic stimulus. It was buried within the huge economic stimulus bill precisely to avoid an open debate about its merits.

The initial stimulus bill that emerged from the House of Representatives had 40% of its spending targeted for 2011 and later, when the crisis would supposedly have passed. Critics thought this odd. They forgot that 2012 would be a Congressional election year, something that the House drafters clearly had in mind. Three Senate Republicans voting for the bill reduced the "out" spending to about 25%. The bulk of the spending both in near and out years went to deficit ridden state and local governments. Of this money, a disproportionate amount went to states controlled by Democratic elected officials.

Congressional Democratic leaders promised that the Stimulus Act would create almost four million jobs. Of course these figures were more or less pulled out of thin air. But even if true, the cost would have been over $200,000 per job,[90] four times what it costs to create an average job in the private economy. And of course the quality of the jobs, and how long they would last after the government's money was spent—well, time would tell. In the event, only a small number of enduring jobs were created if any.*

The idea of stimulus spending to create jobs is closely associated with British economist John Maynard Keynes, who died in 1946. He said that increased deficit spending in a depressed economy would always pay for itself:

> Public works even of doubtful utility may pay for themselves over and over again at a time of severe unemployment, if only from the diminished cost of relief expenditure.[91]

He further elaborated by saying that for each dollar spent, there would be

> at least three or four times[92]

as many dollars of GDP growth and as many as twelve.

Where did these numbers come from? Apparently they came out of thin air. Keynes said at one point to Montague Norman, governor of the Bank of England, that his theories were a

> mathematical certainty, [not] open to dispute,[93]

but that was just a crude bluff.

---

* For more detailed discussion see chapters 15 and 30 from the author's book *Where Keynes Went Wrong: And Why World Governments Keep Creating Inflation, Bubbles, and Busts* (Mt. Jackson, VA: Axios Press, 2011).

Keynesian economists have never been able to document the returns Keynes promised from deficit stimulus spending. They have not even been able to demonstrate conclusively one dollar of GDP growth from a dollar borrowed and spent.

In January, 2008, before Jason Furman was appointed candidate Obama's campaign Economic Policy Director and subsequently Deputy Director of the White House National Economic Council, he wrote that stimulus was "a less effective option" for creating jobs. As he said then,

> the key to economic growth is higher saving and investment to increase the capital stock and thus the productive capacity of the economy.[94]

Christina Romer, President Obama's choice to be his first chairman of the Council of Economic Advisors, also looked at post-war American recessions and found little evidence that fiscal stimulus had helped end them.[95]

As John Cochrane, University of Chicago Business School professor, has concluded,

> I've been looking through graduate course outlines and textbooks, and I can find nowhere in the last 50 years that anybody in economics has said that [deficit spending as a] fiscal stimulus is a good idea. What are we doing giving [such] advice . . . [when] there's nothing [in what] . . . we teach our graduate students that says fiscal stimulus works?[96]

Although stimulus has never provided what Keynes promised, some leading died-in-the-wool Keynesians (e.g. Paul Krugman, Robert Shiller, and even Christina Romer, who was inside the Obama White House) have complained that the Obama Administration just failed to apply enough of it. This is a convenient argument. When the patient dies, you blame the patient for not following doctor's orders perfectly. But when you look back at the Keynesian advice actually provided in 2008, it was never explicit. Robert Shiller said at the time that stimulus "has to be done on a big enough scale [and will be needed] for a long time in the future." Christina Romer added helpfully: "Beware of cutting back on stimulus too soon."[97] No specific amounts or timeframe were provided.

When some Republicans promised that deficit spending produced by tax cuts would magically not only create jobs, but also actually reduce the deficit, these economists called it fanciful. But they continued to think that a deficit caused by more government spending would produce exactly this magic, despite all evidence to the contrary. And these same advisors offered equally vague policy advice for the Fed.

President Obama rarely mentions the word stimulus anymore. He learned from President Hollande of France to refer to stimulus and also to deficit spending simply as "growth." In this way, deficit spending becomes a "growth" policy and opposition to it becomes anti-growth, anti-employment, and anti-middle class. Fortunately Bernie is more honest. He calls for a public works program and a federal jobs program for youth and everyone knows what he means. He does not, however, mention that vanishing interest rates engineered by the Fed and praised by Bernie have encouraged companies to invest in machines rather than people, or that the $3–$5 an hour added to the effective minimum wage by Obamacare, along with new overtime and other rules, has also encouraged employers to automate rather than to hire.

20

Bernie for Workers

Bernie on the Minimum Wage

Why are people working longer hours for lower wages? Enough is enough. We cannot continue to maintain a minimum wage in this country of 7 dollars and 25 cents an hour. That is a starvation wage, and we need to move the minimum wage to a living wage of 15 dollars an hour over the next few years. It is not a radical idea, it is not a radical idea to say that if somebody works 40 hours a week that person should not be living in poverty, that family should not have to be going to an emergency food shelf in order to get food to sustain their family.

July 29 Organizing Kickoff Event, July 29, 2015

THE PROBLEM HERE is that Bernie cannot wave his magic wand and make an employee, especially a young or unskilled and untrained employee, worth a minimum of $15 (plus employment taxes and

Obamacare costs) to any employer. Nor would $10 or $20 or any other number make more sense. There is no logical basis on which Washington can choose a number to impose by law on everyone.

To think otherwise is just wishful thinking, and destructive wishful thinking that could prevent a teenager from getting his or her first job and thus a chance to start moving up. Many teenagers from wealthy families compete to work today as unpaid summer interns in order to get skills, work experience, and credentials. Not surprisingly, the Obama administration does not like internships either and has tried to stop the practice.

Why do politicians such as Bernie favoring a higher minimum wage refuse to consider an exemption for a "training wage"? The short answer is that their union allies (bosses?) forbid it and union endorsed candidates are not brave enough to buck them.

We need only look as recently as the Crash of 2008 to see the damage caused by the federal minimum wage. The rate was raised in steps to $7.25 during and after the Crash. This hurt impoverished, inexperienced young workers the most, so why would anyone be surprised that the teenage unemployment rate rose to 26% in 2009, 39% for black teenagers, and 52% for all teenagers in Washington, DC? Obamacare significantly compounded the problem by adding $2.28–$5.89 of cost per hour for every full-time worker and more for part-time. Applying overtime pay rules to more and more workers further contributed to unemployment.

As this author wrote in *Where Keynes Went Wrong*:

> If an economy is stumbling, and unemployment is high, it means that some prices are far out of balance with others. Wages, for example, may be too high in relation to prices, or prices too low in relation to wages.
>
> Some companies, some industries may be doing well; others may be in desperate straits. What is needed is an adjustment of particular wages and particular prices within and between companies, within and between industries, within and between sectors. These adjustments are not a one-time event. They must be ongoing, as each change leads to another in a vast feedback loop.
>
> In some cases, the wages or other prices should rise. In other cases, they should fall. No single across-the-board adjustment will work. It will just make things worse. The economy is not a water tank to be filled or drained until the right level is reached. Such crude plumbing will not adjust or coordinate anything. It will just make a mess.

Given that the proponents of a higher federal minimum wage generally consider themselves to be Keynesians, it is somewhat ironic that Keynes himself favored uniform wage reductions as a tool to increase employment during hard times, but did not pursue the idea because of what he called enforcement difficulties.[98] Economist

Ken Mayland echoed this in 2010 when he wrote an article entitled "To Create Jobs, Cut Everyone's Pay 10%."[99] But both Keynes and Mayland are misguided; uniform reductions in wages would just cause more trouble precisely because they are uniform. It is not all wages or all prices that need adjustment. It is particular wages and prices. Left alone, the price system will sort it out, restore profitability, and, doing so, both restore and create jobs.

Bernie on Equal Pay for Women

> A living wage should not only be fair, it should be equitable. That is why we must establish pay equity for women workers by law. It's unconscionable that women earn 78 cents on the dollar compared to men who perform the same work.
>
> Southern Christian Leadership Conference,
July 25, 2015

> We need to sign the Paycheck Fairness Act into law. Equal pay for equal work.
>
> United Steelworkers Rally, April 29, 2016

Who would not support the principle of equal pay for equal work? Nor is it easy for employers to thumb their noses at it. Companies pay a significant marketplace penalty if they discriminate based on race or gender or anything else, because they will drive away their best employees or potential employees and damage their reputation with customers.

That said, the figure Bernie cites, that women make 22% less than men, has been shown over and over again by economists to be misleading, as Bernie well knows. Consider a few of the variables known to influence female versus male lifetime earnings, unrelated to the issue of employer gender discrimination. Studies show that women, on average, at least in the past, have tended to work fewer hours, perhaps because they have children to care for, perhaps because they may value their personal life more. Discrimination cannot be ruled out of course. Perhaps fewer hours reflects a greater difficulty getting a job or overtime.

Women have also been more likely, at least in the past, to choose professions, such as teaching, that may offer less upside potential for pay. In addition, women are more likely to enter, leave, and re-enter the labor force for discrete periods of time, for example to raise children. Since experience, skills, and raises all compound over time, the years out of the labor force may significantly reduce the working wage. Studies that have tried to identify men and women without children, of similar age, and working in the same profession have not been able to identify any documentable wage differential.

Bernie on Childcare for Working Parents

> We can live in a country . . . Where every parent can have quality and affordable childcare.
>
> Waterfront Park, Burlington, Vermont, May 26, 2015

Bernie on Universal Pre-K

> Instead of cutting head start and childcare, we need
> to move to a universal pre-k system for all the chil-
> dren of this country.
>
> Des Moines, Iowa, June 12, 2015

Since Bernie supports universal childcare and pre-K, why does he remain silent when national unions try to force homemakers offering childcare for neighboring children to become licensed and to pay union dues, some portion of which will be siphoned off for campaign contributions to the Democratic Party? Neighbors taking care of neighbors would seem to be a far better solution than yet another non-functioning and scandal plagued government run industry. And how much will the neighbors have to charge once they are subject to training and licensing costs and have to pay union dues?

21

Bernie for Medicare for All

Healthcare . . . as a right . . . exists . . . not just
Denmark, Sweden or Finland. It exists in Canada,
France, Germany and Taiwan. That is why I believe
in a Medicare-for-all single payer healthcare system.

On Democratic Socialism in the United States,
November 19, 2015

T HERE ARE LOGICAL problems here. Healthcare
is not like water. When we speak of water, everyone pretty much understands what the word
describes. But what is healthcare? Unlike water, it must
be defined and not only defined but continually redefined based on the latest research.

In a market economy, consumers have the last word
in defining any product. If they buy computers, they are
endorsing the way the word is currently defined by producers. If they do not buy, they are rejecting what the
producer has defined as suitable for them. If healthcare

is a legal "right," then government must define what the word means, and government is incompetent to do so. Government lacks the expertise to decide and all too often is bought and paid for by the existing providers of medical services. These vested interests in medicine will fight tooth and nail for the status quo and against any changes that will cost them money. The consumer's interests are not likely to be considered, much less protected, if healthcare is treated as a legal right guaranteed (and also defined) by government.

There is another gaping logical problem in Bernie's argument. Why does healthcare as a right lead to a Medicare-for-all solution? It certainly does not need to take that direction. Medicare and Medicaid and Veterans medical programs are essentially medical ghettos into which old people and poor people are herded. Why do it this way?

The government addresses hunger in America very differently. The food stamp program gives people cards that look like credit cards and can be used at any store selling groceries, although the Obama administration is trying to restrict convenience stores. The card holder pays the same price as anyone else and chooses whatever he or she wants.

Why does Bernie reject the idea of providing medical assistance for the indigent in the same way? Just give people a medical card and let them buy what they need like anyone else? Why force people to accept a sub-standard product in Medicare and the Obamacare exchange policies, a very substandard product in Medicaid, and—shameful to say—a completely broken product for our military veterans.

Even Medicare medical coverage is poor. It comes with all sorts of restrictions. With the exception of one test per year, your doctor cannot order blood or urine tests unless he or she thinks you are ill. Medicare and Medicaid will also not pay for any conversation by phone or email, will not pay for time spent teaching you how to do anything for yourself, and do not allow the doctor to treat you for two complaints at the same time.

If you have an infection and also high blood pressure, you have to make a second appointment. What Washington bureaucrat dreamed up that rule? And how does this waste of time for everyone make any sense? The object of course is to discourage you from getting too much care, which is a form of unspoken rationing.

For now, Medicare will pay your doctor more than Medicaid, and may pay more than an Obamacare exchange policy, but do not expect that to last. The Obamacare law was partly financed with major cuts to doctors' compensation under Medicare. Perhaps those cuts will never happen, and were just thrown in to pretend that Obamacare would not bust the federal budget. But if the budgeted cuts are ever implemented, expect a mass exodus of doctors from Medicare.

There is a great deal else wrong with Medicare. Basically, it is a system of government price controls, and history has shown that price control programs never work over the long run. In eighteenth century France, price controls on wheat led to bread shortages, mass starvation, and eventually the French Revolution. In America, medical price controls have also caused endless dysfunction and injustice, but have not yet led to a revolution, partly because they remain largely invisible to the public.

Starting with Medicare almost a half century ago, and then Medicaid, the government systematically set out to eliminate market pricing from medicine. Today Medicare relies on recommendations from the American Medical Association (AMA), a government funded player in the crony medical system, to set prices on 7,500 tasks, varied by location, higher if paid to a hospital, and other factors. This means that at least six billion transactions are price controlled at any one time.

Medical insurance companies (which actually run Medicare) then adjust these price controls for their own use. Obamacare has made all these existing price controls even more complicated and dysfunctional. Note also that the Medicare decision to pay hospital employees much more than other doctors for the same service has meant that hospitals have gradually taken over clinical medicine. This works well for the hospitals and the government, which can trade favors with each other, but the resulting local monopolies encourage massive inefficiency, high prices, and lower quality treatments.

A doctor who is unsure of what to charge under Medicare is allowed to call the agency. He or she may or may not get through, but in any case cannot legally rely on the answer. Moreover, getting it wrong can lead to fraud charges and even jail. How did this happen? Here is an explanation from the Alliance for Natural Health-USA:

> Many new laws and regulations were enacted in the 1990s in order to prevent burgeoning healthcare fraud and abuse. Unfortunately these laws do not require criminal intent. A doctor can be prosecuted and sent to jail for an entirely innocent violation of a labyrinth of regulations. Some examples:
>
> ■ The Health Insurance Portability and Accountability Act of 1996 (HIPAA) added anti-fraud provisions providing jail terms of up to ten years. According to the law, if a patient dies while being given a "medically unnecessary" treatment paid for by an outside party and the government decides that the treatment caused the death, the doctor can go to jail for life. Yet even Medicare cannot tell a doctor in advance what it considers "medically unnecessary." This legislation also extended the anti-fraud provisions to cover bills submitted to any "healthcare benefit program." Under federal law, healthcare

benefit programs include private insurance as well as federal programs. So a doctor can go to jail for getting on the wrong side of a private insurance company.

- Medicare and Medicaid rules represent a hopeless minefield for doctors. Some of the laws passed in the '90s were designed to punish cheating both in federal programs and in state programs with any federal financing. The trouble with these laws is their vagueness. "Not medically necessary" and "fraud" are defined the same way, even though they are potentially very different.

- In this way, medical care has become a very high-risk profession. It is also very easy for a doctor to make a false claim. In one experiment, a researcher contacted five different government Medicare billing advisors about a possible claim, and got five different answers about how to handle it. If the government does not know, how can a doctor be expected to know?

What if you want a medical test not covered by Medicare? You could pay for the additional testing, but if those tests are deemed "medically unnecessary," your doctor could go to jail for writing that prescription if he or she bills Medicare for the test. And here is a further Catch-22: it is illegal for your doctor to bill you personally for something that Medicare *does* cover, even though finding out what Medicare does or does not cover may be next to impossible.

You can avoid all these problems by staying out of Medicare. Then your doctor can prescribe what he or she thinks best. But keep in mind that the government will deny you any Social Security payments if you have not signed up for Medicare. Another alternative is to sign up for Social Security, which will automatically enroll you in Medicare A and B, but then tell the government to remove you from Part B. Part A is hospital services, and that is enough to keep your Social Security. Part B covers the doctor's office, and if you don't have it, then the doctor cannot be charged with billing you for services covered by Medicare.

■ This same broken system also discourages technological innovation, since each new test or treatment must not only get FDA approval but also go through the time-consuming process of getting a Medicare billing code and then convince Medicare to actually pay for the service, which is very difficult and often takes many years or even decades.

The irony is that this criminalization of doctors—particularly doctors who favor natural treatments—has done little to actually stop the medical fraud perpetrated mostly by real criminals but also by some doctors.

Based on the above, Bernie's proposal of Medicare for all makes no sense. Perhaps Bernie should concentrate on reforming the woeful medical services offered by the Veterans Administration, then reform Medicare,

Medicaid, and the Obamacare exchange policies before forcing everyone else into Medicare. And, by the way, what would it take to clean up the Veterans Administration? It would require firing some people. But government union work rules will not allow that, which Bernie also refuses to discuss.

22

Bernie for College for All

> It is insane and counter-productive to the best interests of our country, that hundreds of thousands of bright young people cannot afford to go to college, and that millions of others leave school with a mountain of debt that burdens them for decades. That must end.
>
> Waterfront Park, Burlington, Vermont, May 26, 2015

No argument with Bernie on any of the above. He continues:

> That is why, as president, I will fight to make tuition in public colleges and universities free, as well as substantially lower interest rates on student loans.
>
> Waterfront Park, Burlington, Vermont, May 26, 2015

BEFORE WE TRY to evaluate either proposal— to make public colleges, especially community colleges, free, and to lower student loan rates, it might be helpful to review a speech by President Obama on August 22, 2013 in Buffalo, New York that was devoted to the same issues, how best to address the high cost of college and the increasing burden of debt on students.

The president proposed to "reform" the student loan program. He acknowledged that the program has some problems, but assured the audience they are easily fixed. Basically just take the principles behind Obamacare and apply them to education. The president personally "guaranteed" that his proposals would make college more affordable.[100]

Here's the plan the president laid out. The government will rate colleges based on fees (the lower the better) and graduation rates (the higher the better) and student success in finding a job. Then student loan funds will be allocated to schools according to the rating. Students will also be guided to the best-rated schools via government web sites. And schools will get more funding if they set up demonstration projects to reduce costs. This will all encourage more "competition" among schools. Yes, you heard that right: more government control of colleges will increase market "competition."

There is no 2,000 page bill in Congress yet, but it's all quite familiar: government will take even tighter control of higher education just as it has taken even tighter control of medicine, and use Obamacare as its operating manual. Of course, Obamacare not only rated medical insurance policies; it mandated what would be in them at what prices, which in effect put government in charge of defining what healthcare is. Presumably, the government rating of schools will in due course also lead to mandates and the government defining what higher education is.

There is a lot more in common between Obamacare and Obamaschool than these superficial characteristics. Obamacare came into being because of a crisis in medical care. As usual, that crisis had been caused by earlier government interventions in medicine, especially its Medicare price controls, which have been adopted by the insurance companies running Medicare for private policies as well. There really is no longer any private medicine: it is all part of a government/corporate crony system.

As government has come to dominate medicine and price-control it, prices have inevitably risen at a rate that threatens to bankrupt the economy. Obamacare has doubled down on the price controls and required a price control board, although the board has not even been appointed yet, many years after the law's enactment. All of this will no doubt lead to the kind of legislation recently passed in Massachusetts where any "material" change in a medical practice, in either prices or services, must be approved by the state.

Obama was proposing to apply his government medical services model to higher education for similar reasons. In this case, the government set up a student loan program that was ostensibly intended to subsidize students. But whenever government subsidizes demand without increasing supply, prices inevitably rise, and this was no exception. In effect, the subsidy intended for students was instead going to the schools, which could use the subsidy to avoid having to adopt cost controls.

As President Obama pointed out:

> Over the past three decades, the average tuition [and fees] at a public four-year college has gone up by more than 250 percent. *250 percent*. Now a typical family's income has gone up 16 percent. That's a big gap.

Yes it is.

In reality, both the 250 percent and the pitiful 16 percent have been caused by government policies, especially price manipulations and controls. The 250 percent increase in fees (mitigated somewhat by increases in student aid) has specifically been driven by government's mistake in flooding schools with student loan money.

That money did not help students; it just led to higher and higher fees. What students mostly got out of the loan program was an early initiation into massive debt. If leaving school with heavy debts is not exactly slavery, it certainly represents some kind of indentured servitude.

Obama was more than a bit mendacious about this debt burden. He took credit for keeping student interest rates down. He even said that "government shouldn't see student loans as a way to make money; it should be a way to help students." But the reality is that his administration currently borrows money at negligible interest rates and then relends it to students at much higher rates. The difference is booked elsewhere in the federal budget under "deficit reduction." If that is not a clear case of using student loans as a way to make money for the government, then what is? It would appear that in this case the president lied through his teeth.

What would really happen if the federal government ever completed a takeover of higher education pricing? The certain result would be even higher prices, which would then lead to calls for a complete federal takeover, just as advancing prices under Obamacare are now leading to admissions by Senator Reid and Congresswoman Pelosi that it was only intended to be a stepping stone to a "single payer" system in which government in effect nationalizes all healthcare. Nationalizing healthcare would make the crisis worse, not better, but Reid and Pelosi don't understand that. Nationalizing public higher education would also make the crisis there much worse.

The president's specific proposals for student loans would have other unintended effects as well. If schools get more federal money as their graduation rate increases, they will simply stop taking students who are more likely to drop out. That of course means they will stop taking disadvantaged students who need help the most.

The administration says that it would get advice from schools in devising the rating system. This is all we need: closed door meetings in Washington between the government and special interests with the consumer excluded. This is exactly how Mussolini ran Italy and Roosevelt tried to run the US with the National Recovery Act. The results of dismantling a consumer-driven market economy will be no better now than they were then.

Back to Bernie on free college tuition:

> Some of our young people have given up the dream of going to college, while others are leaving school deeply in debt. Many of the countries we compete with understand that free public education should not end at high school. In many European countries, students leave college debt free. That should be the case here in our country.
>
> National Association of Latino Elected and Appointed Officials Conference, June 19, 2015

As our discussion of President Obama's proposals for ending the spiraling student debt burden suggests, Bernie is simply ignoring the unintended effect of student loans in ballooning the cost of college. If the government just doles out unlimited funds to higher education, whether in grants or student loans, why should higher education ever make the changes it needs to make to become affordable again?

The government gave colleges a blank check in the form of unlimited student loans, and most of the money did not help the students. It just went into more salaries, more administrative personnel unconnected to teaching, often unconnected even to education ("diversity counselors"), and more and bigger performing arts centers and athletic facilities. Meanwhile the students are being destroyed by debt and arguably get little direct benefit from the education.

Four year residential colleges were founded in ages past primarily for youths of rich or at least connected families. We need an entirely new model for disadvantaged and middle class youths today, but will not be able to move in a new direction if we just subsidize an increasingly bloated old model.

We have all heard stories of useless courses developed by faculty members with swollen egos or political agendas. Bernie is absolutely right that students should not face a lifetime of debt to pay for such frivolous services, but throwing money at the problem will just make it worse, not better. And the federal takeover of public education that will inevitably follow the free tuitions will also make things worse, not better. Crony education is already a troubling issue because of the steady flow of money back and forth between academe and Washington. Do we really want to make that worse?

Here is just one example of crony education. The Obama administration correctly observed that for-profit schools were exploiting the student loan program, so began a regulatory crackdown and also launched a series of legal investigations of these schools, including the largest such school, the University of Phoenix. The pressure on for-profit schools made the administration's "war" against coal companies seem tame. Consequently the stock price of the Apollo Group, owner of the University of Phoenix, fell by over 80%.

Marty Nesbitt, reportedly President Obama's best friend and frequent golfing buddy, chairman of the Obama Foundation, which will build the president's library, and a very rich businessman evidently saw an opportunity in the share price collapse of the University of Phoenix's owner. He stepped in and put together a group, including a former Obama administration Department of Education official, to buy the Apollo Group for $1 billion in cash. The seller was no doubt assured that by taking this step, the school's legal and regulatory nightmare would end. The selling family might also have suspected that worse tortures would await if the Nesbitt offer were declined.

This is only one of innumerable examples of the same thing. Another is the way that drug companies, supported by Washington, have virtually taken over university medical research. Everything done by all parties is legal, as determined by hordes of sharp lawyers, but the university/Big Business/Washington triangle of cronies just gets stronger with each passing year.

This rarified world of prestigious universities, Wall Street high finance, and Washington power brokers seems far removed from the state universities and modest community colleges that Bernie wants to subsidize. But maintaining the independence and integrity of all of higher education, while forcing it to face facts, accept change, and discipline its budgets, is essential for the future of the entire country, not just young people who are currently being fleeced by their purported guardians.

What we really need are online degrees that are honestly priced and truly cheap. Today many online programs are rip-offs designed to make the companies marketing them rich. We also need ways for young people to socialize and meet and learn from each other that are also reasonably priced and do not require residence in a country club atmosphere.

Do not expect government to provide any sensible answers. More likely, government will use its subsidies and other powers to protect today's vested interests and thwart any change that threatens the income of those vested interests, whether they are companies, unions, schools, school faculties, or others. If anyone will push through the needed innovations and changes, it will be educational entrepreneurs backed by consumers.

Bernie on student loan rates:

> It's a little bit crazy that someone who has student debt is paying 8, 9, 10 percent in interest rates, when they can refinance their home today for 2, or 3, or 4 percent. So we have got to let people who have

that student debt to refinance at significantly lower interest rates. Second part of that is that the United States government should not be profiteering off of the high interest rates of the student debt working families have. So we have got to end profiteering on the part of the government. We do those two things, we substantially lower student debt interest rates in this country. . . . That is why, as president, I will . . . substantially lower interest rates on student loans.

July 29 Organizing Kickoff Event, July 29, 2015

On this point, Bernie is absolutely correct so far as he goes but does not go nearly far enough. What interest rate would be charged? What rate would he deem no longer "profiteering"? The answer should be the same rate the federal government pays. Anything more will encourage government costs to rise to absorb the subsidy. Let general tax funds pay the administrative costs of the program and keep those costs down; only charge our young people the bare minimum, which should be what the government itself pays.

23

Bernie for Open Borders

I believe in a path to citizenship, and I agree with President Obama's plans to do through executive action what the Congress refuses to do through legislation.

Des Moines, Iowa, June 12, 2015

THIS IS TROUBLING because it violates the Constitution, as a federal court and then a divided Supreme Court found in the case of President Obama's orders to open our borders. Immigration laws are supposed to be made by Congress. And once legislation has passed, administration officials should not be able to refuse to enforce it, as the Obama administration has repeatedly and brazenly refused to enforce immigration restrictions. President Obama took a sworn oath to defend and protect the Constitution and the laws and no president should be able to disregard what he has sworn to do.

This is a fundamental principle that is completely independent of what we think our immigration laws should say.

If government officials promote and practice disrespect for the rule of law, who will guard us from the guardians? Bernie may feel that acting lawlessly is justified in this case, but how would he feel if political opponents, with far different ends, began acting the same way?

Cynical observers worry that President Obama's actions have been motivated more by politics than by real conviction. If they were motivated by real conviction, why did he wait so late in his presidency to issue executive orders on this issue? If the motivation was simply political calculation, it was shrewd, in that taking these actions forced the Republicans either to accept it or risk alienating Hispanics, the single fastest growing voting group.

It was truly a Catch-22 for Republicans. If they accepted it, there would be millions of new voters, most of them expected to vote as Democrats, and all the more likely to do so after the president's actions. If they opposed it, they would alienate millions of existing voters. Insofar as Obama's orders triggered the revolt among Republican voters that led to the successful primary campaign of Donald Trump, the president might be particularly pleased. He had in effect thrown a grenade into electoral politics and it had gone off inside the

Republican Party. On the other hand, the whole thing has the potential to backfire, if the majority of voters, including many Hispanics, became sufficiently aroused against immigration to turn against Democrats.

And it was not just President Obama who appears to have been making these same calculations. After Obama's re-election in 2012, the strongest candidate for 2016 among the Republicans appeared to be Senator Marco Rubio of Florida. Indeed given how close Romney came to winning in 2012, it is possible that Rubio, running as the first Hispanic candidate for president, might have won that year, had he entered the race.

In 2013, Senator Chuck Schumer persuaded Rubio to join him in what became the "gang of eight" immigration bill in the Senate. Schumer almost certainly thought that Rubio's sponsorship of the bill, which provided a path to citizenship, would prove to be a poison pill for Rubio among Republican primary voters, especially since Rubio had taken a stance against open borders or amnesty when he ran for the Senate. Schumer's crafty maneuver succeeded in destroying Rubio's presidential prospects.

Rubio tried to recover, but was never able to extricate himself from the Schumer bill. A possible approach would have been to say that he had only supported and voted for the bill to prevent what he thought would be illegal executive orders from President Obama. There was a basis for this: he had said something like it at the time. This might have enabled him to make a clean break with the Democrat's bill.

Instead he seemed to half defend and half reject what he had done, and claimed in debates that Senator Ted Cruz had adopted pretty much the same position he had, which was patently false. This did not extricate him from his mess, but instead made it worse.

About Schumer's bill, which he voted for, Bernie told a meeting of the immigration activist group La Raza:

> This is not to say that I do not have significant criticisms of this long and complicated bill. I believe the pathway to citizenship was unnecessarily linked to border security triggers, measures that many believe were put in place so that the path to citizenship would be delayed or even denied for the millions of undocumented individuals here and I want to change those provisions. I also believe that the penalties and fines in the bill would be a bar for the poor, essentially preventing them from accessing the path to legal residency and eventual citizenship. . . . These and other barriers in the bill, including the years, often more than a decade, that it would take to achieve citizenship make it a flawed piece of legislation and needs to be improved. . . .

> National Council of La Raza, August 12, 2015

Bernie is especially opposed to building a physical barrier on the border:

> I also opposed tying immigration reform to the
> building of a border fence.
>
> National Association of Latino Elected and
> Appointed Officials Conference, June 19, 2015

Bernie clearly favors an open border and an immediate path to citizenship for anyone who crosses it, legally or illegally. In the meantime:

> As President, . . . I will direct immigration officers
> to immediately stop initiating deportations against
> those eligible for relief. This would include: disman-
> tling inhumane deportation programs and private
> detention centers, enhancing access to justice, and
> reversing the criminalization of immigration.
>
> . . . I will [also] direct my Administration to extend
> humane treatment and asylum to victims of do-
> mestic violence and unaccompanied minors com-
> ing from Latin America as a distinct group of peo-
> ple fleeing persecution.
>
> Fair Immigration Reform Movement
> Strategy Summit, November 9, 2015

In addition to the problem of proposing more executive orders and continuing to bypass Congress, which clearly has legal authority over immigration, an additional problem with Bernie's immigration proposals is that they seem logically inconsistent with his pledges to restore the American middle class and raise wages for the poor and all other workers. We have already noted in an earlier chapter that it is odd for Bernie to want to wall off products made by impoverished foreign workers abroad in order to protect American jobs, but to welcome any numbers of foreign workers to the US, where they would compete even more directly with current US workers.

Bernie has pointed out in speeches to Latino groups that twelve million Latinos or one in four currently live in poverty. He does not explain why open borders would not further depress their job and pay prospects. Bernie acknowledges that:

> Many [Hispanics] in poverty are working at low-wage jobs.
>
> National Association of Latino Elected and
> Appointed Officials Conference, June 19, 2015

Julia Hahn writing in *Breitbart* offered a very thorough analysis and critique of this seeming contradiction:

> Harvard Professor George Borjas has explained [that] "the negative effect [of open borders] on native-born black and Hispanic workers is significantly larger than on whites because a much larger share of minorities are in direct competition with immigrants. . . ." Borjas' analysis has shown that "a 10% immigrant-induced increase in the supply of a particular skill group is associated with a reduction in the black wage of 2.5%, a reduction in the black employment rate of 5.9 percentage points, and an increase in the black institutionalization rate of 1.3%."

"Competition from immigration accounts for approximately 40 percent of the 18-percentage point decline in black employment in recent years," US Civil Rights Commissioner Peter Kirsanow has documented. "That's nearly a million jobs lost by blacks to immigrants." Borjas has highlighted the writings of economist Paul Samuelson, [a progressive icon] who in 1964, observed that "... By keeping labor supply down, immigration policy tends to keep wages high. ..."

The historic [increase in the] flow of [legal] immigration into the United States is primarily the product of a Ted Kennedy-supported immigration law enacted in 1965, which lifted immigration caps that had been put into place during the Coolidge administration, and opened immigration to predominantly poor and developing countries.

Every year the US admits one million plus foreign nationals on green cards, one million guest workers, dependents, and refugees, and half a million foreign students. [Excluding the students, this totals to 59 million new residents since 1965.] In 1970, fewer than one in 21 Americans was foreign-born. Today, as a result of the federal government's four-decade-long green card gusher, nearly one in seven [legal] US residents was born in a foreign country. ...

Recent reports have documented the sustained compression of the middle class during the forty-year green card wave, as well as the discovery that all net job creation among working-age people went to foreign workers from 2000–2014. . . .

[In support of the earlier Coolidge administration restrictions on legal immigration,] American Federation of Labor (AFL) founder and president Samuel Gompers . . . said, "Those who favor unrestricted immigration care nothing for the [American] people. . . . "

In 2007, Senator Bernie Sanders opposed George W. Bush's expansive immigration agenda because it would "bring low-wage workers into this country in order to depress the wages of American workers, which are already in decline." Sanders wrote: "With poverty increasing and the middle-class shrinking, we must not force American workers into even more economic distress. The CEOs who want this [immigration] bill aren't even embarrassed by their hypocrisy."[101]

This reference to corporate CEOs' desire for more or even unlimited immigration suggests that Bernie may actually oppose legal immigration while proposing open borders for illegal immigration. This is very odd indeed. Hahn also notes that

full amnesty for the illegal immigrant population will cost US taxpayers $6.3 trillion, according to a report from the Heritage Foundation. Similarly, Clinton's plan to resettle 65,000 Syrian migrants would cost US taxpayers over $42 billion over the course of the migrants' lifetime. Donald Trump recently called on

Clinton "to replace her support for increased refugee admissions . . . with a new job program for our inner cities. We have to use the money to take care of our poorest Americans and work with them, so they can come out of this horrible situation that they're in."

Bernie on Refugees

Both Bernie and Hillary propose to accept a large number of Syrian refugees, and have repeatedly spoken in favor of keeping borders open for all refugees. About this, political analyst Roger L. Simon has written:

> Earth to elites: Citizens of truly democratic countries don't want unlimited immigration into their countries by people who couldn't be less interested in democracy.[102]

24

Bernie for Criminal Justice Reform, Marijuana Legalization, GMO Labeling, and against Global Warming and War

Bernie for Criminal Justice Reform

We—the United States of America—have more people in jail than any other country on earth. We have more people in jail than China which is an authoritarian state with a population many times our own. And we should lay it all right out on the table. People in American jails are disproportionately people of color. That's the reality in America today. That's a reality that has to change.

. . . One in every 15 African-American men is incarcerated, compared to one in every 106 white men. . . .

> We must end the over incarceration of non-vio-
> lent young Americans who do not pose a serious
> threat to our society.
>
> Presidential Justice Forum at Allen University,
> November 21, 2015

BERNIE IS RIGHT. The American criminal justice system needs a thorough reform; the over-
reliance on jail needs to end. But Bernie needs
to go further. How will he actually accomplish this?

One proposal that he does not mention is to use
Marine Corps style "boot camps." A short stay in a
boot camp could be offered first time and/or non-violent offenders as an alternative to a much longer prison
sentence. Boot camps should be just as tough as they
are in Marine training. They should build physical
condition, enforce discipline, teach how to get up in
the morning and report to work at a fixed time, and if
possible teach some actual employment skills.

This kind of training can build self-esteem as well as
well as self-discipline. Politicians are currently afraid
to tackle criminal justice reform in a meaningful way.
It is past time to do it, and to offer concrete proposals, not just rhetoric, even if the rhetoric is accurate, as
Bernie's largely is.

Bernie is also critical of local police departments.
In effect, he blames them for some of the problem
of too many blacks in prison. But, again, he leaves
out an important part of the story. To reform police

departments, it is essential to give department chiefs the power not only to hire but to fire officers. Union work rules generally make this very difficult. Bernie as usual will not criticize unions, especially public unions, and so does not explain how police departments can be managed effectively.

This issue is mirrored in schools as well. How can we expect public schools to be well managed if principals lack the authority to fire as well as hire teachers? But the public unions which Bernie supports uncritically prevent this.

Bernie again:

> Thirteen percent of African-American men have lost the right to vote due to felony convictions.
>
> Presidential Justice Forum at Allen University,
> November 21, 2015

An issue that needs to be addressed here is the present linkage of voting rights and gun purchase rights. In 2016, Governor Terry McAuliffe by executive order restored the voting rights of 206,000 convicted felons in Virginia. He reportedly did so because he was convinced that most of these people would vote for his party. The Supreme Court struck down this order on the grounds that the decision belonged to legislators. Critics also noted that the order allowed convicted felons to begin a process that would enable them to buy guns.

It does not make sense for voting and gun rights to be merged in this way. Ironically, it is Democrats such as McAuliffe who want to reduce or eliminate gun sales, and who have proposed refusing sales to a much wider category of persons, such as those on the "no fly" list.

The problem with this proposal is that there is no due process for the "no fly" list. People may find themselves on it just because of confusion over a name. It might also be counter-productive to alert people that they are on the FBI "watch list." But there are other ways to accomplish this, such as immediately notifying the FBI and providing for further review before a sale is made.

> We also have to develop standards and crack down on communities that are using their police forces essentially as revenue generators. . . . Communities that receive an inordinate amount of their local funding through fines and citations need to be stopped.
>
> Presidential Justice Forum at Allen University,
> November 21, 2015

This is a real issue, and we should be grateful to Bernie for mentioning it. When police officers are given revenue quotas for tickets, they cease to be guardians of public safety and instead become predators whose personal interests are not aligned with that of the public. Not long ago, the policeman in the neighborhood was often regarded as everyone's friend and protector.

Governments may not be able to recreate that, but
they can at least stop destroying it.

> We have to make sure poor communities have ac-
> cess to credit on fair terms, so they can buy homes,
> start business, and avoid predatory lenders.
>
> Presidential Justice Forum at Allen University,
> November 21, 2015

This is also a vital issue. Predatory lending is ravag-
ing poor communities and creating a new kind of slavery. In some cases, public officials operate a side business that does the lending and then demand to receive
the government welfare check directly. Very little
of the government money ever reaches the intended
recipient, and if the person caught in this web fails to
vote as the public official demands, there is implied or
actual retaliation. All of this adds up to the worst kind
of corruption. Bernie should say exactly what he proposes to do about payday lending and all the abuses
that accompany it.

> We need to end mandatory minimum sentencing
> and give judges the discretion to better tailor sen-
> tences to the specific facts of a given case.
>
> Presidential Justice Forum at Allen University,
> November 21, 2015

Yes, but if we go back to giving judges a large amount
of sentencing discretion, we had better at least have
maximum sentencing rules.

Bernie for Marijuana Legalization

> It is time to take marijuana off the federal list of controlled substances and let states decide whether they want to go forward with legalization, regulation and taxation without interference from the federal government.
>
> Presidential Justice Forum at Allen University,
> November 21, 2015

Newer research suggests that marijuana use might interfere with memory and other brain functions more than previously thought. But that does not mean its use should be a federal crime. As in prohibition, that just vastly enriches criminals and destroys public safety. This would seem to be an educational issue rather than a criminal one.

Bernie does not mention it, but a close marijuana relative, hemp, is also prohibited from being grown under federal law. Since hemp does not produce the effects of marijuana, is one of the best sources of plant protein, has a good omega 3 to 6 fat ratio, and is allowed to be imported from foreign countries (primarily Canada) and sold in grocery stores, the federal ban on planting is nonsensical. The only conceivable argument is that it can be hard to distinguish hemp and marijuana plants from the government helicopters, but this can be temporarily addressed by requiring a publicly recorded license to grow it or, better still, by taking the federal government out of the marijuana control business.

Bernie for Labeling Genetically Modified (GMO) Food

Vermont passed legislation requiring food producers to let consumers know if the food in their products was genetically modified. The effective date of the legislation was July 1, 2016. Big Food companies had spent many millions beating back such bills in California and elsewhere by falsely claiming that such a labeling requirement would increase the cost of food, and were aghast that tiny Vermont had succeeded in upsetting their GMO apple cart. (Yes, there is a GMO apple.)

Big Food responded by obtaining bi-partisan legislation in Congress that overruled Vermont and provided for "labeling" that could be effectively hidden in obscure bar codes, in tiny type, that most consumers would never be able to read. This law was sponsored by Senator Roberts of Kansas, a Republican, and Senator Stabenow of Michigan, a Democrat. It passed with overwhelming support, and was just the last in a series of proposed "Dark Acts" designed to keep the American public in the dark about what was in their food. Bernie has been a keen advocate of labeling and fought hard against the various dark acts and for full disclosure to consumers.

Bernie against Global Warming

> When we talk about our responsibilities as human beings and as parents, there is nothing more important than leaving our planet healthy and habitable for our kids and grandchildren.

> Des Moines, Iowa, June 12, 2015

Who would disagree? Bernie continues:

> The debate is over. The scientific community has spoken in a virtually unanimous voice. Climate change is real. It is caused by human activity and it is already causing devastating problems in the United States and around the world.

> Des Moines, Iowa, June 12, 2015

Opposition to climate change is one of Bernie's most passionate positions. He reiterates his concern and what he proposes to do about it over and over again. One has to wonder, however: If he thinks the scientific community is virtually unanimous about it, why not leave this to the scientists and the press? Why make it a partisan, political position? Why not try to achieve a political consensus in both parties, which cannot happen with so much partisanship?

Before Bernie, the principal American spokesman against global warming (now climate change) was Al Gore, who ran for president as a Democrat in 2000. He was a famous and articulate spokesman, but by embracing his leadership, the environmental community also embraced extreme political partisanship. Was that a wise choice? As a result, many Republicans think that global warming is a Democratic plot to gain partisan advantage, and nothing else.

Republicans and other critics also dismiss Obama administration claims that the Paris Accord on climate change was epochal, viewing it instead as a very expensive measure that will have little or no effect on carbon emissions. Scientist Bjorn Lomborg has noted that the UN's climate model shows only a 0.08 degree improvement from the Paris measures by the end of the century. Clearly, if global warming is to be prevented, much, much more would be needed.

Bernie again:

> The scientists are telling us that if we do not boldly transform our energy system away from fossil fuels and into energy efficiency and sustainable energies, this planet could be five to ten degrees Fahrenheit warmer by the end of this century. This is catastrophic. It will mean more drought, more famine, more rising sea level, more floods, more ocean acidification, more extreme weather disturbances, more disease and more human suffering. We must not, we cannot, and we will not allow that to happen.

> Des Moines, Iowa, June 12, 2015

> The United States must lead the world in reversing climate change. We can do that if we transform our

energy system away from fossil fuels, toward energy efficiency and such sustainable energies such as wind, solar, geo-thermal, and bio-mass. Millions of homes and buildings need to be weatherized, our transportation system needs to be energy efficient, and we need a tax on carbon to accelerate the transition away from fossil fuel.

Waterfront Park, Burlington, Vermont, May 26, 2015

"Sin" taxes such as on cigarettes or as proposed on carbon emissions may have unintended effects. If government becomes dependent on the revenue, as it inevitably does, it may lead to a situation where government actually protects the activity, while pretending to try to end it.

Green investments or subsidies may also backfire if they are government financed. President Obama's green energy investment program became a way to reward major campaign donors with grants and cheap financing, and thus a shameful example of crony capitalists helping themselves to a government honey pot, with scandalous results of lost jobs and wasted taxpayer money.

Bernie against War

As everybody knows, we live in a difficult and dangerous world, and there are people out there who want to do us harm. As president, I will defend this nation—but I will do it responsibly. As a member of Congress I voted against the war in Iraq, and that was the right vote. I am vigorously opposed to an endless war in the Middle East—a war which is unwise and unnecessary. We must be vigorous in combatting terrorism and defeating ISIS, but we should not have to bear that burden alone.

Waterfront Park, Burlington, Vermont, May 26, 2015

[In combatting international terrorism] . . . we should be part of an international coalition, sustained by Muslim nations, which can not only defeat ISIS but also begin the process of creating conditions for a lasting peace. America has and will continue to shoulder the burden that is the cost of freedom at home and around the world, but that burden must be shared by other nations who have the resources and means to protect themselves and their corner of the earth.

Des Moines, Iowa, June 12, 2015

Most Americans would presumably agree, but these remarks do not reveal much of what Bernie would actually do as president either in his foreign policy in general or in combatting the threat of terrorism. In this respect, they seem uncharacteristically evasive, raise more questions than they answer, and contrast with Bernie's detailed disclosure of his positions on domestic policy.

Part Eight

Conclusion

25

Bernie for Big New Ideas

Now is not the time for thinking small.

Southern Christian Leadership Conference,
July 25, 2015

We can deliver . . . change, but we can't do it by tinkering with the system at the margins. We need to think bigger and bolder if we are going to deliver the kind of social and economic transformation that we are all demanding.

Presidential Justice Forum at Allen University,
November 21, 2015

We have an economic and political crisis in this country and the same old, same old establishment politics and economics will not effectively address it.

On Democratic Socialism in the United States,
November 19, 2015

> Now is not the time for the same-old, same-old establishment politics and stale inside-the-beltway ideas.
>
> Southern Christian Leadership Conference,
> July 25, 2015

WHEN BERNIE SPEAKS about thinking big and taking bold action, it rings true. When he speaks of new ideas and "new economic models," it rings completely false. Bernie's ideas are very old, as old as Roosevelt and Johnson, and really over a century old. As noted earlier, he resembles nothing so much as a Fabian Socialist from the late nineteenth century in Britain.

Bernie's ideas do not represent an escape from "stale inside-the-beltway" ideas; they have been common currency among progressive circles in Washington since at least the 1930s. They are not forward looking, but backward looking.

In effect, Bernie is fighting for a massive expansion of policies that have already been tried over and over again. Given that he himself thinks we have now arrived at a crisis moment, it defies logic to think that the policies that brought us to this moment just need to be reaffirmed and adopted on a much broader scale in order for us to succeed. Bernie is right that we need new ideas and approaches, but he is not offering any.

Bernie states that:

As Pope Francis made powerfully clear last year in Laudato Si', we have the technology and know-how to solve our problems—from poverty to climate change to healthcare to protection of biodiversity. We also have the vast wealth to do so, especially if the rich pay their way in fair taxes.

The Urgency of a Moral Economy: Reflections on the 25th Anniversary of Centesimus Annus, April 15, 2016

Bernie often returns to this theme of how rich in production, technology, and money the United States is, and how these should enable us to help the poor and middle class. He seems not to understand how any of these assets are created, and blithely assumes that he can tax the producers at very high rates without impairing their production at all.

Even if this were possible, it is not clear how the extra taxes would really help the poor and middle class, since the immediate beneficiaries would be government employees. Government employment has been the leading growth industry in the US for a long time, and very little of that money "trickles down" to those in need.

More, much more government is Bernie's answer for just about everything. Here he not only refers to Pope Francis, but quotes him approvingly:

While the income of a minority is increasing exponentially, that of the majority is crumbling. This

> imbalance results from ideologies which uphold
> the absolute autonomy of markets and financial
> speculation, and thus deny the right of control to
> States, which are themselves charged with provid-
> ing for the common good.
>
> The Urgency of a Moral Economy: Reflections
> on the 25th Anniversary of Centesimus Annus,
> April 15, 2016

Public officials may be charged with providing for the common good, but more often provide for their own good. Established to guard us from predation and parasitism, they all too often resort to predation or parasitism of their own. Giving government more and more control over the economy and over our lives will not fix anything, as the history of the last century and last few decades of repeated bubble and bust demonstrate.

The more control government has over the economy, the more incentive exists for crony capitalism to thrive, and the corruption of crony capitalism is rotting our economy and society. This is all plain enough to see. The issue of how big government should be and how far it should intrude into the economy is not "outmoded" as *New York Times* columnist David Brooks has suggested.[103] It is still the pivotal question, and a call for yet more government is the old and stale position.

Unfortunately Bernie does not see this. He is forever wedded to the socialist ideas of his long ago youth in Brooklyn, although as we have noted, he does seem to have swung from being suspicious of what open borders do to the wages of working people to an embrace of ever more immigration, perhaps because he hopes that will produce the Democratic voters who will finally bring the realization of his program of government commanding everything.

Meanwhile at least some voters in democracy are getting fed up. Writing about the British vote to leave the European Community, economist Larry Kudlow has argued that

> if you look under the hood of the populist revolt in Britain, and the budding revolts in larger Europe and America, the anger is in good part rooted in the lack of economic, job, and wage growth. Worldwide, growth has been missing. All the major countries have been operating under big-government spending, heavy regulations, and the insane central-bank policies of QE and zero (now negative) interest rates. It hasn't worked. Middle-income wage earners have had enough.[104]

David Brooks has written that the question of how much government is "archaic."[105] He meant no longer relevant, which is false, but it is true that the debate about whether government intervention into the economy helps or hurts is indeed very old. Bernie's ideas do not really date even to the nineteenth century. They have flourished for thousands of years and thwarted human economic progress all along the way.

Ancient Chinese annals tell us that the Han Dynasty emperor Wu-di (155–87 BCE) decided that government must control the economy, and castrated his advisor Sima Qian for daring to dispute his view. Although Wu-di said that he was setting up monopolies granted by the state in salt, iron, and other basic commodities in order to protect the common people from greedy merchants, his monopolies really just made a few merchants colossally rich, and ensured a steady stream of kickbacks from them to court officials and to the Emperor himself.*

Almost two thousand years later, the Scottish economist Adam Smith restated Sima's case in words strikingly reminiscent of the early Chinese master's own:

> The natural effort of every individual to better his own condition, when suffered to exert itself with freedom and security, is . . . not only capable of carrying on the society to wealth and prosperity, but of surmounting a hundred impertinent obstructions with which the folly of human laws too often encumbers its operations.[106]

In the meantime, the middle and later Roman emperors imitated Wu-di. They granted monopolies,

---

* Some of the facts and text for this chapter are drawn from chapter 16 from the author's book *Are The Rich Necessary? Great Economic Arguments and How They Reflect Our Personal Values, Updated & Expanded Edition* (Mt. Jackson, VA: Axios Press, 2009); also from chapters 24 and 29 of the author's book *Free Prices Now! Fixing the Economy by Abolishing the Fed* (Edinburg, VA: AC2 Books, 2013).

instituted price controls punishable by death, debased the currency by stripping precious metals from coins, exacted ever harsher taxation, and reaped a whirlwind of corruption and economic collapse. As economist Jesus Huerta de Soto has written: "Roman civilization did not fall as a result of the barbarian invasions." It undermined itself from within through its own economic policies, although serious plagues also played a part in decimating and demoralizing the population.[107]

In Sung China (tenth century, CE), merchants were classed with undertakers and other "unclean" groups,[108] and the government did not hesitate to confiscate mercantile fortunes that came to its attention, a pattern that persisted throughout Chinese imperial history. The great historian of commerce and capitalism, Fernand Braudel, acknowledges that

> in the vast world of Islam, especially prior to the eighteenth century, ... ownership was temporary, for there, as in China, [property] ... legally belonged to the prince. ... When the [rich person] ... died, his seigneury and all his possessions reverted to the Sultan of Istanbul or the Great Mogul of Delhi. ...[109]
> [In addition,] André Raymond's recent study of eighteenth century Cairo shows us that the great merchants there rarely were able to maintain their positions for more than a generation. They were devoured by political society.[110]

The historian David Landes records the same thing in Japan. He cites the case of Yodoya Tatsugoro, scion of the leading commercial family in Osaka. The family had made itself immensely rich, had also performed many services to the nation, and had regularly lent money to the ruling classes. These loans could not be refused, but once made, they led to strained relations. In the end, all the family's money was confiscated by the government on the grounds that Yodoya was "living beyond his social status."[111]

Looking at the long millennia in which the human race made little or no enduring progress against poverty, British economist John Maynard Keynes (died 1946) made the rather foolish claim in his famous *General Theory* that

> the destruction of the inducement to invest by [a tendency to keep what wealth one had under a mattress] was the outstanding evil, the prime impediment to the growth of wealth, in the ancient and medieval worlds.[112]

What Keynes seems to have intentionally omitted from his account was that people hid their money because they feared theft, and they especially feared theft by government.

When economic conditions finally began to improve in the nineteenth century, first in Britain and then in America and elsewhere, it was because at least a few governments had learned that it is better to let private capital accumulate, that it is wiser to pluck the goose of private enterprise than kill to it. Lord Macaulay correctly observed that, at least in Britain,

> profuse government expenditure, heavy taxation, absurd commercial restriction, corrupt tribunals, disastrous wars, ... persecutions, conflagrations, inundations, have not been able to destroy capital so fast as the exertions of private citizens have been able to create it.[113]

Keynes simply ignored all this in his fanciful suggestion that twentieth century governments would decide economic issues based on "long views, ... the ... general social advantage[,] and ... collective wisdom."[114] He concluded that "state planning, ... intelligence and deliberation at the center must supersede the ... disorder [of the past]."[115]

It is notable that Keynes was not entirely consistent about this perverse and completely unrealistic advice. He insisted that the future was unknowable, but seemed to forget this when extolling the "long views" of state planners. He also acknowledged the "muddle" that poor state policy choices had on occasion produced,[116] and even at one point referred to politicians and even other economists as "utter boobies," thereby anticipating humorist P. J. O'Rourke's remark that "bringing the government in to run Wall Street is like saying, 'Dad burned dinner, let's get the dog to cook.'"[117]

The collapse of the Soviet Union put some tarnish on Keynes's dream of economic control from "the center." By the late 1990s, Harvard economic historian David Landes, a person of common sense, wrote that: "[All] sides blithely assume that free markets are in the saddle and riding the world."[118] But this was simply a mirage.

As economic writer James Grant noted:

> Central planning may be discredited in the broader sense, but people still believe in central planning as it is practiced by [The US Federal Reserve]. . . . To my mind the Fed is a cross between the late, unlamented Interstate Commerce Commission and the Wizard of Oz. It is a Progressive Era regulatory body that, uniquely among the institutions of that era, still stands with its aura and prestige intact.[119]

Economist William Anderson was even more critical:

> Central banking, for all its "aura," is no less socialistic than the Soviet Union's Gosplan [the Soviet agency charged with creating Communist Russia's economic plan].[120]

Bernie has his issues with the Fed, but not with the idea that it should centrally plan our economy.

British statesman William Churchill quipped that "a politician needs the ability to foretell what is going to happen tomorrow, next week, next month, and next year. And to have the ability afterward to explain why it didn't happen."[121] Based on this observation, Fed officials and other government officials charged with economic management are not good economists, but they are good politicians.

Journalist Walter Lippmann, in general a spokesman for modern progressivism, noted a curious paradox in his and Bernie's belief that government direction of the economy will make it better:

> This is the vicious paradox of the gradual collectivism which has developed in western society during the past sixty years: it has provoked the expectation of universal plenty provided by action of the state while, through almost every action undertaken or tolerated by the state, the production of wealth is restricted.[122]

There is a further paradox here not mentioned by Lippmann. Fearful of private greed, wanting what is best for all, progressives bring government into ever more minute management of economic as well as political affairs. But in doing so, they do not strengthen our community. Instead they create an epidemic of lying, cheating, theft, and corruption, with more and more people trying to get something for nothing, relying not on what they can do, but on whom they know in government. In surprisingly little time, all the bonds of trust and cooperation nurtured by the free price system become frayed or just disintegrate.

26

Bernie's Dilemma

BERNIE IS OFTEN described as a populist. In many respects, he fills the bill. But we have to remember what populism is and is not.

Franklin Roosevelt infamously redefined the meaning of the word *liberalism* in the 1930s to mean more and more government control of the economy. This was in complete contradiction to what the word had meant for centuries, as defined by people like Jefferson: less government control of the economy.

Now some advocates of more government control over the economy are arguing that Donald Trump is a populist. This is odd. A reasonable definition of a populist is someone who wants what is best for the poor, the middle class, and ultimately all Americans (the Latin root of the word means the people). By definition, a populist is someone who is not working on behalf of himself or herself or other special interests. Since most government officials are closely allied with special interests, this leaves out most government officials.

Donald Trump certainly does not appear to be a populist. When asked why he had praised the Clintons and contributed to their campaigns in the past, before bashing them now, he replied that as a successful businessman he had sought to befriend all politicians, because they controlled his fate as a real estate developer. This is the essence of crony capitalism, not populism.

Progressives have been known to dismiss Trump supporters as a "mob." The word mob gives them away. They are probably elitists themselves, the opposite of populists. If they call Trump a populist, they do not mean it as a compliment.

Describing Bernie as a true populist, which he clearly intends to be, does not mean that only his supporters can be grouped under this banner. In America today, there are two wings of populism, one led by Bernie, who sees in government the solution for every problem, even the problems created by government, and another led by former Congressman Ron Paul, who thinks exactly the opposite.

Sanders and Paul often agree in identifying issues, such as an elitist and misguided Federal Reserve. But they always disagree about the solution. In contrast to Bernie, Ron Paul thinks, with hard-to-fault logic, that you cannot cure the depredations of crony capitalism, an alliance of special interests with government, by giving more power to government.

Bernie does not much use the term populist to describe himself. He generally calls himself a socialist or a progressive. Nobody but Bernie thinks these two terms are identical, although one wit has described progressivism as "timed release socialism."

When Bernie describes his socialism, it does not really sound like socialism, which usually implies government ownership of all or much of the economy. By this definition, something like Amtrak, the government owned passenger rail service, is run on socialist lines, while industries controlled by government, but not owned by it, are run on progressive lines.

Critics of progressivism label this kind of tight government control of the economy without ownership fascism. They have a point. This is exactly how Mussolini and Hitler operated. But then, to confuse matters further, Hitler called himself a "national socialist."

Here is what Bernie says about his socialism:

> The next time you hear me attacked as a socialist, remember this: I don't believe government should own the means of production.

> Democratic socialism means that our government does everything it can to create a full employment economy. . . .

> Democratic socialism means that, in the year 2015, a college degree is equivalent to what a high school

degree was 50 years ago . . . [and] every . . . [quali-
fied] person in this country [should have] the right
to go to a public college or university tuition free.
[This also extends to healthcare, retirement assistance, and so forth.]

Democratic socialism means that we must reform
a political system in America today which is not
only grossly unfair but, in many respects, corrupt.

On Democratic Socialism in the United States,
November 19, 2015

One does not have to be a socialist to agree with
Bernie that the American system has become corrupt.
Ron Paul would agree. So does the author of this book.

As noted above, Bernie calls himself a progressive
more often than a socialist:

I am a proud progressive, prepared to stand with
the working families of this country; prepared to
take on powerful special interests which wield enormous power over the economic and political life
of this country.

New Hampshire Democratic Party Convention,
September 19, 2015

To bring people together we need a simple and
straight-forward progressive agenda which speaks
to the needs of our people, and which provides us
with a vision of a very different America.

Waterfront Park, Burlington, Vermont, May 26, 2015

What are we to make of this? Progressivism as a political movement began with one simple idea. Special interests in the form of rich people and corporations had too much power and were using it to the detriment of ordinary people. Progressives would deploy the power of government to regulate and quell these special interests.

As we have seen, this idea proved false in at least two respects. First unions, trial lawyers, universities, even churches, all ostensible allies of the progressives, could be just as selfish as rich people or corporations. Government itself all too often acted as a special interest in its own right and preyed on the very public it was supposed to protect.

The modus operandi of progressivism was to give ever more power to government, especially power over the economy. This backfired because it gave special interests ever more incentive to try to befriend and even buy off government for their own purposes. Crony capitalism, the merger of special interests with government, had always been with us. As we have seen, President Andrew Jackson attacked it in the 1830s when he abolished our national central bank of the time. Progressivism just made crony capitalism much worse.

How do today's progressives react to these doleful realities? Some of them simply join the crony capitalist game. We see this in:

- Progressive teachers who mainly focus on getting higher pay or who talk up a lottery for education, even though lotteries generally take money from those who have the least

- Progressive union members fighting against jobs going to anyone outside the union

- Progressive seniors who do not mind being subsidized by young people who are on average the poorest group of all

In these instances, the alleged reformers may be talking the old talk, but they seem to have found a comfortable spot in the crony capitalist system. They have traveled a long distance from what may have been the idealism of their youth, still mirrored in the young people who intensely protest against what they call "capitalism," communicating through their iPhones, digging up "activist" information on the internet with iPads, or meeting up at Starbucks to recharge with very costly varieties of caffeine, all with little or no perceived irony, but at least with a still untainted sincerity. Bernie too remains sincere, but he has not "sold out" in this way.

Other progressives think that the answer is just to cut the poor and middle class in at least a little more, to give them a bigger slice of the crony capitalist pie. In this view, the entire purpose of politics is not to reform the system or fundamentally change it, but rather to get more for your voters, at the expense of other politicians and voters. It is essentially a "spoils system," and where it has gone wrong is that the poor and middle class have gotten too little of the spoils.

Columnist George Will regards this as nonsense. He writes that

> [progressives] have a rendezvous with regret. Their largest achievement is today's redistributionist government. But such government is inherently regressive: It tends to distribute power and money to the strong, including itself.
>
> Government becomes big by having big ambitions for supplanting markets as society's primary allocator of wealth and opportunity. Therefore it becomes a magnet for factions muscular enough, in money or numbers or both, to bend government to their advantage.[123]

How then can government be expected to restrain the special interests with which it is so closely allied, on whom it so greatly relies? How can money and power be prevented from flowing back and forth between private interests and government through ever more polluted channels? How can we prevent average citizens from always getting the short end of the stick, as they did so memorably during and after the Crash of 2008.

Progressive thinkers deal with this issue in different ways. Most simply deny the problem. The *Economist*

magazine, itself generally progressive, criticized leading progressive (and Keynesian) economist Joseph Stiglitz for taking this easy tack of denial:

> After [Stiglitz] has condemned today's policymak-
> ers so roundly as incompetent and beholden to spe-
> cial interests, [his] prescription [for] better regu-
> lation . . . and [his] broader faith in government
> activism sounds perverse. If policymakers failed as
> miserably as Mr. Stiglitz believes, then he ought to
> be far more worried about the potential for govern-
> ment failure in the future. That dissonance is a glar-
> ing weakness in Mr. Stiglitz's [position].[124]

So it is. And it is an equally glaring weakness for Bernie, who like Stiglitz, simply refuses to acknowledge the
dilemma or explain what he proposes to do about it.

The logical answer is to restrict the power of government, to keep it out of a command role in the economy, in particular to leave pricing decisions entirely
to private companies. In that way, the benefits to be
gained from crony arrangements between private interests and government will be greatly reduced, and so
will crony capitalism.

This is the original vision of the American founders. Government powers would be divided between
the president, Congress, and the courts in order to
safeguard against tyranny. Neither the executive nor
Congress would ever be permitted to borrow and print
money without limit. The founders did not explicitly

forbid this because they never imagined that any government would dare to claim this power. Even Alexander Hamilton, apostle of a stronger national government, firmly opposed the idea of paper money. He said that it would just lead to "bubble" and bust. What he failed to add was that crony capitalism thrives in conditions of government created bubbles.

In the founders vision, government would not be barred from the economy. It would be needed to pass and enforce the rules of the economic game, act as umpire, provide courts, but never act as manager of our economic life. This is still a good plan for any country. It is too bad that a sincere populist such as Bernie does not see that the life of the poor and middle class cannot be improved by expanding government's control over the economy, but only by reining it in to appropriate limits.

Every living society, even societies of microorganisms, reveals a mix of competition, cooperation, predation, and parasitism. Especially in our human society, the challenge is to increase healthy competition within an overall framework of cooperation while barring predation and parasitism. By putting government more and more in charge of the economy, we are vastly increasing the chances that government will cease to be the umpire we need and instead become a predator or parasite itself, with disastrous consequences for all of us, but especially for the poorest and weakest among us.

Endnotes

1. *Newsweek* (November 9, 1981): 108.
2. P. J. Proudhon, *What is Property* (1840).
3. Quoted by Malcolm Deas, "Catholics and Marxists," in *London Review of Books* (March 19, 1981); also in P. T. Bauer, *Reality and Rhetoric: Studies in the Economics of Development* (Cambridge, MA: Harvard University Press, 1984), 79.
4. Julius Nyerere, *The Economic Challenge* (London: 1976); also in Bauer, *Reality and Rhetoric*, 79.
5. *Free Market* (March 2003): 5.
6. Wilhelm Röpke, *Economics of the Free Society* (Chicago: Henry Regnery Company, 1963), 10.
7. Henry Hazlitt, *The Failure of the "New Economics": An Analysis of the Keynesian Fallacies* (New Rochelle, NY: Arlington House, 1978), 246.
8. Henry Hazlitt. *The Conquest of Poverty* (Irvington-on-Hudson, NY: Foundation for Economic Education, 1994), 227-28.
9. Ibid., 234.
10. Ibid., 228.
11. Ludwig von Mises, *Economic Policy: Thoughts for Today and Tomorrow* (Lake Bluff, IL: Regnery Gateway, 1985), 1.

12. *Forbes* (October 6, 2003): 60.

13. *Forbes* (October 11, 2004): 52.

14. *New York Times* (July 20, 1992): D-1; and *Forbes* (April 21, 1997): 112.

15. Thomas Sowell, *Forbes* (January 30, 1995): 81.

16. E. F. Schumacher, *Small is Beautiful: Economics as if People Mattered* (New York: Harper & Row, 1973), 36.

17. *In These Times* (December 8, 2003): 12.

18. P. T. Bauer, *Equality, the Third World, and Economic Delusion* (Cambridge, MA: Harvard University Press, 1981), 9.

19. Ibid., 10.

20. Joseph Alsop, *I've Seen the Best of It* (New York: W. W. Norton, 1992), 473.

21. John Maynard Keynes, *The General Theory of Employment, Interest, and Money* (London: Macmillan, 1936), 374, 376.

22. Norman Cott, *Free Market* (January 2003): 7.

23. *Forbes* (March 16, 1992): 64.

24. A World Bank estimate. See *World Development Report 2000/2001: Attacking Poverty* (Oxford, 2001); also cited in Rebecca Blank, *Is the Market Moral?: A Dialogue on Religion, Economics, and Justice* (Washington: Brookings Institution Press, 2004), 39.

25. Friedman, *Capitalism and Freedom*, 169.

26. Friedman, *Free to Choose*, 137.

27. Steve H. Hanke, "Kowtowing to Capitalism's Enemies," *Forbes* (August 6, 2001): 77.

28. Ibid.

29. Hazlitt, *Conquest of Poverty*, 51.

30. Arthur Okun, *Fortune* (November 1975): 199.

31. Irving Kristol, "'Business' vs. 'The Economy,'" *Wall Street Journal* (June 26, 1979): Op Ed.

32. Ikeda, *Dynamics of the Mixed Economy*, 180.

33. *1994 Economic Report of the President*, President's Council of Economic Advisors.

34. Ted Honderich, *After the Terror* (Edinburgh: Edinburgh University Press, 2002), 137–38; cited in *Mises Review* 9, no. 1 (Spring 2003): 15–16.

35. Mark Kurlansky, *Cod* (New York: Vintage Books, 2004), cited in *Marathon Global Investment Review* (August 31, 2004): 2.

36. Karl Marx and Friedrich Engels, *The Communist Party Manifesto* (1848).

37. Mises, *Human Action*, 721.

38. Henry Hazlitt, *The Wisdom of Henry Hazlitt* (Irvington-on-Hudson: Foundation for Economic Education, 1993), 86.

39. Lester Brown press release, November 6, 2001.

40. Röpke, *Economics of the Free Society*, 235.

41. See, for example, Rhys Isaac, *Landon Carter's Uneasy Kingdom* (Oxford: Oxford University Press, 2004).

42. Howard Zinn, Emeritus Professor of History, Boston University and author of American history texts and other books, internet interview by David Barsamion, Boulder, CO, November 11, 1992.

43. Mises, *Economic Policy*, 3.

44. Milton Friedman, *Capitalism and Freedom* (Chicago: University of Chicago Press, 1962), 170.

45. Milton and Rose Friedman, *Free to Choose: A Personal Statement* (New York: Avon Books, 1981), 138.

46. Paul Johnson, *Will Capitalism Survive* (Washington, DC: Ethics and Public Policy Center, 1979), 4; also

in Michael Novak, *The Spirit of Democratic Capitalism* (New York: Madison Books, 1982), 121.

47. A term coined by Michael Polanyi (1951); also see Sanford Ikeda, *Dynamics of the Mixed Economy: Toward a Theory of Interventionism* (London and New York: Routledge, 1997), 256 passim.

48. Friedrich Hayek, "The Use of Knowledge in Society," *American Economic Review*, 35:4 (September 1945): 519–30. Reprinted in F. A. Hayek, *Individualism and Economic Order* (Chicago: Henry Regnery, 1972), 77–91.

49. *Economist* (September 28, 1996): 28.

50. *Weekly Standard* (February 25, 2002): 19.

51. Marcia Angell, "The Truth About Drug Companies," *New York Review of Books* (July 15, 2004): 52.

52. John Maynard Keynes, *Essays in Persuasion* (New York: W. W. Norton, 1963), 372.

53. Ayn Rand, *Atlas Shrugged* (New York: Signet, 1957), 415.

54. Ayn Rand, *Capitalism: The Unknown Ideal* (New York: Signet, 1967), 29.

55. Friedman, *Capitalism and Freedom*, 164–65.

56 Adam Smith, *The Wealth of Nations* (Edinburgh, 1776), bk. 1, chap. 2, 20.

57. Ibid., bk. 4, 352.

58. David S. Landes, *The Wealth and Poverty of Nations: Why Some Are So Rich and Some So Poor* (New York: W. W. Norton, 1999), 402.

59. Walter Lippmann, *The Good Society* (Boston: Little Brown and Company, 1943), 193–94; also in Novak, *Spirit of Democratic Capitalism*, 100.

60. S. Jay Levy, and David Levy, *Profits and the Future of American Society* (New York: Mentor Books, 1984), 125.

61. George Stigler, *The Intellectual and the Market Place*, (Glencoe, IL: Free Press, 1963); also in Denis Thomas, *The Mind of Economic Man* (Kent, UK: Quadrangle Books, 1970), 148.

62. Geoffrey Martin Hodgson, *Economics and Utopia* (New York: Routledge, 1999), pt. III, 256; also in McCann, *Elgar Dictionary*, 75.

63. Letter to editor of Smith College campus newspaper, *Forbes* (July 21, 2003), 52.

64. To check the math, see Sowell, *Basic Economics*, 272–74.

65. *Forbes* (September 20, 2004): 43; citing study by Global Insight (USA).

66. Julia Hahn, http://www.Breitbart.com (June 25, 2016).

67. http://www.cnn.com (January 15, 2015).

68. *New Statesman and Nation, Collected Writings* Vol. 20 (March 16, 1931): 502.

69. Interview, *New York Magazine* (December 28, 2015).

70. J. S. Mill, *Essays on Some Unsettled Questions of Political Economy* (1830, 1844); also in Henry Hazlitt, *Failure of the "New Economics": An Analysis of the Keynesian Fallacies* (New Rochelle, NY: Arlington House, 1978), 367.

71. *New York Times* (January 19, 2010).

72. Bernanke's Obfuscation, http://www.economonitor.com, a Roubini Global Economics Project (December 9, 2011).

73. *Bloomberg News* (July 20, 2009), detailing report of Neil Barofsky, special inspector general of Federal TARP (Troubled Asset Relief Program) designed to rescue banks and other financial institutions.

74. http://www.bloomberg.com (January 25, 2013).

75. Friedrich A. Hayek, *Monetary Theory and the Trade Cycle* (London: Jonathan Cape, 1933), 21–22.

76. Ibid., 18.

77. *The New Yorker* (September 21, 2009): 60.

78. http://www.politico.com (December 23, 2015).

79. Adam Smith, *The Wealth of Nations*, bk. IV, chap. 2 (Edinburgh, 1776); also in G. Bannock, R. E. Baxter, and R. Reef, *The Penguin Dictionary of Economics* (London: Penguin Books, 1972), 247.

80. M. Deane and R. Pringle, *The Central Banks* (London: Hamish Hamilton, 1994), n.p.; also in James Grant, *The Trouble with Prosperity: The Loss of Fear, the Rise of Speculation, and the Risk to American Savings* (New York: Times Books, 1996), 198.

81. President Jackson's veto message regarding the Bank of the United States: (July 10, 1832), http://www.avalon. law.yale.edu.

82. House Ways and Means Committee, May 1939, quoted in Burton Folsom, *New Deal or Raw Deal? How FDR's Economic Legacy Has Damaged America* (New York: Threshold Editions, 2008); quoted Charen, http:// www.nationalreview.com (November 25, 2012).

83. *Washington Times* (September 17, 2012): 34.

84. Paul Johnson, *Modern Times: The World from the Twenties to the Eighties* (New York: Harper & Row, 1983), 229.

85. *Forbes* (September 10, 2012): 14.

86. Shostak, http://www.mises.org (October 18, 2012).

87. Thomas Sowell, http://www.townhall.com (December 12, 2012).

88. *Weekly Standard* (February 23, 2009): 5.

89. *Washington Times* (February 2, 2009): 35.

90. *Weekly Standard* (April 15–20, 2009): 14.

91. Keynes, *General Theory*, 127.

92. Keynes, *Collected Writings* (vol. 21), 326.

93. Keynes, letter to Norman, May 22, 1930, in *Collected Writings* (vol. 20), 350–56; cited in Skidelsky, *John Maynard Keynes* (vol. 2), 351.

94. *Brookings Institution Paper* (January 2008).

95. For a review of Romer's work on stimulus, see Edward L. Glavser (a Harvard economist), "Today's Economist," http://www.nytimes.com (December 2, 2008).

96. http://www.chicagomaroon.com (February 3, 2009).

97. Robert Shiller, *Bloomberg News* (April 16, 2009); Heidi Przybyla, *Bloomberg News* (April 2, 2009), Christina Romer quoted.

98. Keynes, *General Theory*, 264, 267.

99. http://www.marketwatch.com (August 16, 2010).

100. This analysis of the Obama speech first appeared in http://www.lewrockwell.com under the title "Move Over, Obamacare. Here Comes Obamaschool."

101. Julia Hahn, http://www.Breitbart.com (June 22, 2016).

102. http://www.PJMedia.com (June 23, 2016).

103. *New York Times* (July 1, 2016).

104. Larry Kudlow, http://www.RealClearMarkets.com (June 25, 2016).

105. Ibid.

106. Smith, *Wealth of Nations*, bk. IV, ch. 5.

107. http://www.mises.org/daily/6141 (August 23, 2012).

108. "From Yao to Mao," taped lecture.

109. Fernand Braudel, *Afterthoughts on Material Civilization and Capitalism* (Baltimore: John Hopkins University Press, 1977), 73.

110. Ibid., p. 74.

111. Sakudo, Management Practices, 150–51, 154; cited in Landes, *Wealth and Poverty of Nations*, 362.

112. Keynes, *General Theory*, 351; also quoted in Hazlitt, *Failure of the "New Economics,"* 184.

113. Thomas Macaulay, *History of England (1848)*, vol. 1, chap. 3; quoted in Henry Hazlitt, *Economics in One Lesson* (San Francisco: Laissez Faire Books, 1996), 15.

114. Keynes, *General Theory*, 164; and *Collected Writings* (vol. 21), 145.

115. Keynes, BBC Broadcast (March 14, 1932), in *Collected Writings* (vol. 21), 86.

116. Keynes, BBC Broadcast, in *Collected Writings* (vol. 20), 325.

117. *Weekly Standard* (January 19, 2009): 20.

118. Lindsey, *Against the Dead Hand*, xi.

119. J. Grant, interview, *Austrian Economics Newsletter*, 16, no 4 (Winter 1996): 2–3.

120. William Anderson, *Free Market* (June 2003): 6.

121. *Washington Times*, (June 25, 2012): 29.

122. Lippmann, *Good Society*, 119.

123. Will, http://www.washingtonpost.com (January 5, 2012).

124. *The Economist* (March 20, 2010): 91.

Index